A TIME TRAVELLER'S GUIDE TO

OUR NEXT TEN YEARS

★ ★ ★ ★ ★ ★ ★ ★

FRANS CRONJE

Tafelberg

Tafelberg
An imprint of NB Publishers, a Division of Media 24 Boeke (Pty) Ltd
40 Heerengracht, Cape Town
www.tafelberg.com
© Frans Cronje (2014)

Cover design: Simon Richardson
Book design: Cheymaxim
Editing: Riaan de Villiers
Proofreading: Lesley Hay-Whitton
Indexing: Sanet le Roux

Printed and bound by Interpak Books, Pietermaritzburg
First edition, first impression 2014

Product group from well-managed forests and other controlled sources.

ISBN: 978-0-624-06866-2
Epub: 978-0-624-06867-9
Mobi: 978-0-624-06868-6

CONTENTS

ACKNOWLEDGEMENTS

I could not have written this book without drawing heavily on the work and insights of many people and organisations, and without the assistance and support of many others. I am particularly grateful to:

Professor André Duvenhage at North West University, who supervised my doctoral thesis on which this book is based, and his assistant Simone Roos.

Arina Muresan and Carol Archibald, who edited the thesis, and checked all the sources.

Riaan de Villiers, who edited this book, and provided many valuable ideas and suggestions in the process.

Dr Anthea Jeffery and John Kane-Berman, senior colleagues at the Institute of Race Relations (IRR). I have drawn extensively on their ideas and their work.

The library and research team at the IRR, who produced almost all the data I use to substantiate the scenarios, and actively hunted for missing pieces of information.

Louis van der Merwe of the Centre for Innovative Leadership for his advice and support over many years, and particularly for his assistance in developing the final set of scenarios that appear in this book.

South African scenario guru Clem Sunter, for listening to my ideas, providing advice and support, and writing a foreword.

Annie Olivier, my publisher at Tafelberg, who approached me with the idea for this book, and (calmly) guided the process through various drafts through to publication.

I have obviously been inspired by scenario pioneers and experts such as Pierre Wack, Kees van der Heijden, Bill Ralston, Charles Thomas, Peter Kennedy, Patrick Marren, Charles Perrottet, Ian Wilson, Gill Ringland, and especially Peter Schwartz. They have created a rich, new intellectual universe, which I have been privileged to draw on.

Finally, I would like to thank the business people who have invited my colleagues at the Centre for Risk Analysis (CRA) and me into their boardrooms to help them come to grips with South Africa's uncertain future. They were effectively the guinea pigs for our early ideas, methods and scenarios, and I hope they will derive some satisfaction from the knowledge that their investment in the CRA and the IRR has contributed towards this book.

Frans Cronje

FOREWORD

Travelling in time with Frans Cronje is a truly educational experience. He journeys through the next ten years in South Africa using scenario planning as a vehicle to visualise the possibilities we may encounter as citizins.

This method assumes that the future is too complex to reduce to a single prediction, particularly as you go further into it – and ten years is a long trip. Cronje also describes the 'butterfly effect', which is 'the notion that, when a butterfly flaps its wings on one side of the world, it could cause a storm on the other side'. He gives an example of how a monstrous traffic jam is often caused by the breakdown of a single vehicle. Likewise, a small event can change the complete outcome of a complex system.

Hence, as this book beautifully demonstrates, looking at the future is all about reducing the complexity inherent in it, but at the same time revealing the wide range of different paths it can take. This Cronje does by using a ten-step approach, which starts by deciding what you want to achieve. In this case, it is to give readers a feel for what it will be like to live in South Africa in 2024.

To kick off the actual process, he describes the current environment we inhabit – political, social, and economic. He then moves on to analysing the major role players and various policy frameworks developed over recent years. Next, he makes a list of significant trends that are consolidated into a number of highways, each with its own road signs. Then, based on impact and uncertainty, he selects the two major driving forces that can be used to design a matrix. This matrix is used to develop four scenarios in the final section of the book. Crucially, for each scenario he paints a vivid picture of how you get from here to the 2024 world of there, fulfilling the aim of giving people a taste of what they will experience in every one of them.

Without giving too much away – because the book is a thrilling read – I can reveal that the two key variables chosen by the author are on the one hand whether we remain an open, democratic society, or whether we turn into a more authoritarian state with restricted liberties; and on the other whether our economy is largely deregulated against the background of an improving education system, or whether it becomes centrally directed while education remains poor. The interaction between these two variables produces four scenarios: a 'Wide Road', a 'Narrow Road', a 'Rocky Road', and a 'Toll Road'.

Interestingly, when the Anglo American team did the High Road/Low Road scenario exercise in the mid-1980s, they maintained there were two crossroads ahead. The first was a political crossroads where South Africa either became a proper democracy or experienced rising levels of conflict, culminating in a wasteland. The second was an economic crossroads where we either developed an open, free and inclusive economy to match the democracy we had achieved, or continued with a closed, exclusive, and highly regulated economy that ran the risk of undoing all the good work resulting from taking the High Road politically.

We are now at that second crossroads, and there can be no better time for a book of this nature to be published. It will enrich the debate on how we can convert the political miracle into an economic miracle as well. By drawing on his extensive experience at the South African Institute of Race Relations, Frans Cronje has ensured that South Africa will remain at the forefront in the field of scenario planning. More importantly, his scenarios may tip the odds in favour of the country, fulfilling the great potential that it currently possesses.

Clem Sunter

ACRONYMS AND ABBREVIATIONS

ANC	African National Congress
AsgiSA	Accelerated and Shared Growth Initiative for South Africa
BEE	black economic empowerment
BRICS	Brazil, Russia, India, China, South Africa
CBD	central business district
CEO	chief executive officer
CIA	Central Intelligence Agency
COPE	Congress of the People
COSATU	Congress of South African Trade Unions
CRA	Centre for Risk Analysis
DA	Democratic Alliance
DP	Democratic Party
DTI	Department of Trade and Industry
EFF	Economic Freedom Fighters
GDP	gross domestic product
GEAR	Growth, Employment and Redistribution
IEC	Independent Electoral Commission
IFP	Inkatha Freedom Party
IRR	Institute of Race Relations
LSM	Living Standards Measure

MP	member of parliament
NDP	National Development Plan
NDR	National Democratic Revolution
NGP	New Growth Path
NP	National Party
NNP	New National Party
NWU	North West University
OPEC	Organization of Petroleum Exporting Countries
RDP	Reconstruction and Development Programme
SACP	South African Communist Party
SAHRC	South African Human Rights Commission
SAIIA	South African Institute of International Affairs
IRR	South African Institute of Race Relations

THE CURSE OF
RISING EXPECTATIONS

★ ★ ★

On 10 April 1993, at a highly sensitive stage in South Africa's constitutional negotiations, a Polish right-winger named Janus Walusz shot and killed Chris Hani, leader of the South African Communist Party (SACP), in the driveway of his home on the East Rand, provoking fears of widespread unrest. Three days later, Nelson Mandela, then president of the recently unbanned African National Congress (ANC), made the following extraordinary appeal during an address broadcast on national television and radio:

> Tonight I am reaching out to every single South African, black and white, from the very depths of my being. A white man, full of prejudice and hate, came to our country and committed a deed so foul that our whole nation now teeters on the brink of disaster. A white woman, of Afrikaner origin, risked her life so that we may know, and

bring to justice, this assassin. The cold-blooded murder of Chris Hani has sent shock waves throughout the country and the world. … Now is the time for all South Africans to stand together against those who, from any quarter, wish to destroy what Chris Hani gave his life for – the freedom of all of us.[1]

On 17 June 1992, about ten months previously, 40 residents of the Joe Slovo informal settlement in the township of Boipatong in the Vaal Triangle had been hacked to death by hostel dwellers belonging to the Inkatha Freedom Party (IFP), a rival party to the ANC, resulting in the ANC suspending its participation in the constitutional negotiations. And on 28 March 1994, less than a month before the first democratic elections, 19 members of the IFP, many armed with spears and shields, were fatally shot outside Shell House, the ANC's national headquarters in the Johannesburg central business district (CBD), prompting the government to declare a state of emergency across much of the East Rand and Natal. Indeed, my colleague at the South African Institute of Race Relations (IRR) Dr Anthea Jeffery estimates that about 20 000 people were killed in political conflict in the decade before South Africa's first democratic elections.

South Africa seemed to face a dark and uncertain future. Even if the country managed to avoid a civil war, many doubted whether the ANC, a socialist liberation movement long supported by the Soviet Union, could possibly govern South Africa. Boardrooms and dinner parties were rife with fears that the new government would wreck the economy by expropriating land and nationalising key industries such as mining, thus destroying the middle classes.

Fast forward to the present, and we know that the ANC has not ruined the economy, or turned South Africa into a third-world basket case. Neither have we descended into civil war. In fact, life in the suburbs continues as it has done for decades, with braai smoke rising around swimming pools. Shopping centres have proliferated, and are more opulent than ever. Coffee shops have opened in Johannesburg's CBD along the route of the 1994 Shell House march, and the high-end food and clothing retailer Woolworths recently opened a branch a few blocks away. The ANC government has abandoned many of its socialist ideals, and has built a high-speed rail link to ferry business people from the glittering business metropolis of Sandton to the newly refurbished OR Tambo international airport, bristling with shops and restaurants in sharp contrast with the stark concrete air terminal maintained under apartheid.

For years, suburban dinner parties were dominated by conversations about violent conflict and the spectre of socialism; today, the heat is provided by government's attempts to instal an electronic tolling system on Johannesburg's upgraded freeways. This is an extraordinary outcome, considering that some of our fellow countrymen stocked up on shotgun ammunition and tinned food ahead of the 1994 election.

Return to the night when Mandela begged the nation 'from the very depths of my being' to remain calm, and ask what it would have been worth to you – as the country teetered on the edge of an abyss – to know things would actually turn out over the next 20 years. Go back further to the infamous Rubicon speech of 15 August 1985 when then State President PW Botha waved his finger at the world and declared that the apartheid regime would not bow to reformist pressures. The Cold War was at its height. White conscripts were patrolling the townships, and fighting Cubans in Angola. The notion that, 20 years later, the last leader of the National Party (NP) would be the minister of tourism in an ANC government was simply unimaginable, requiring a chain of events that almost every analyst would have classified as impossible.

But the impossible has happened. And South Africa is not unique. The recent upheavals in North Africa that led to the collapse of the governments of Tunisia, Libya, and Egypt caught the whole world by surprise, bucking trends that had kept the governments in those countries in power for decades. The trouble, as the American scenario consultant Ian Wilson has put it, is that: 'However good our futures research may be, we shall never be able to escape from the ultimate dilemma that all our knowledge is about the past, and all our decisions are about the future.'[2] Put differently, we face the seemingly impossible challenge of developing an understanding of the future that is as sound as our knowledge of what has happened in the past.

Questions about our future

For even though we avoided the abyss 20 years ago, we remain concerned about the future. Perhaps it is the discomfort of living in a highly unequal society. Perhaps it is the fear that the transition of 1994 did not go far enough, and that the real revolution still lies ahead. Perhaps we believe that the uncomfortable truce struck between the (largely black) government and (largely white) middle class may not hold.

Over the past five years, my colleagues at the Centre for Risk Analysis (CRA) – the Institute of Race Relation's consulting arm – and I have made hundreds of presentations to corporations, government departments, and foreign diplomats on the likely evolution of South Africa's future. In July and August 2013 alone, two major mining companies, one automobile manufacturer, a prominent chamber of commerce, and a European embassy asked us whether we thought South Africa had enough of a future to make it worth investing in. The word 'disinvestment' is being heard for the first time in 15 years.

The questions we increasingly confront in the course of our interactions with these sorts of role players are also asked by more and more ordinary members of our society. Will the increasingly angry poor rise up and seize land, homes, and businesses? Will we ever be free of the fear of violent crime? Will a desperate government sacrifice our democracy in order to help it cling to power? May middle-class South Africans have to flee the country, carrying little more than the clothes on their backs? Is there any reason we will not go the way of Zimbabwe?

Will the ANC survive three more elections, or will it be swept from power in events as dramatic as those in Tunisia, Egypt and Libya? Can the Democratic Alliance (DA) under Helen Zille defeat the ANC at the polls? What would life be like under a DA-led government? How seriously should we take Julius Malema and his Economic Freedom Fighters (EFF)? Could people with these sorts of sentiments rise to power, and what would the consequences be?

Will the media remain free? Will property rights be respected, or will the state seize our farms? Will there still be good schools and universities to send our children to? What are the prospects for our children to find work and pursue careers? Will the services provided by the government improve, or will they go into terminal decline? If we have the chance to leave the country, should we take it and build new lives and careers overseas? Occasionally, a particularly insightful individual will ask whether growing socio-economic pressures may force the ANC government to adopt economic reforms that will place the country on a more prosperous economic trajectory.

These questions are not only being asked by members of the elite and middle class. One of the perks of my job is that I am called upon to present briefings on the future to a hugely diverse range of people and groupings, from khaki-clad farmers in Mpumalanga to militant youth activists in the Johannesburg CBD. While they view the country in very different ways, they all ask the same questions – although they seldom believe me when I say that their concerns are shared by those whom they see as the 'other side', and even as 'the enemy'.

A decade hence, will our middle classes still be lounging around their braai fires and swimming pools, saying how silly it was to worry that we might go the way of North Africa or Zimbabwe? Or do we need to start making a Plan

B in anticipation of a second, and far less benign, political transition?

The crisis of rising expectations

The answers to these questions will be determined by trends in our economic, social, and political environments. For instance, if the economy performs very badly, expectations among the disadvantaged about rising standards of living will not be met. Should they have the means to do so, they may take steps to change the way in which the country is governed. Should the economy perform well, and meet expectations of rising standards of living, those same people may seek to maintain the status quo. Even a cursory examination of these trends shows that the questions raised about South Africa's stability are not idle ones.

A point of departure for much of our analysis is that – contrary to popular opinion – significant progress has been made since 1994. However, as we will see later, this very progress has become part of the problem, as it has created what we describe as a crisis of rising expectations. On the economic front, for example, South Africa has managed to recover from the low growth and high debt and deficit levels racked up in the 1980s and 1990s. After dipping into negative territory in the early 1990s, the economy rebounded after 1994, averaging gross domestic product (GDP) growth of more than 4% in 2000-2008 and more than 5% in 2004-2007.[3] Inflation dropped from double digits in the late 1970s to 3-6% for much of the post-2000 period,[4] and the prime interest rate by more than half from the levels preceding South Africa's transition.[5] The annual change in gross fixed capital formation, or fixed investment into for instance factories, rebounded into positive territory after 1994, having sat at negative levels since 1982.[6]

Despite weakening considerably against the American dollar in 2001-2002, the rand has (until recently) been relatively stable, especially when compared with the extremely volatile currencies that have wrecked a number of post-colonial African economies – with Zimbabwe a notable recent example.[7] Between 2003 and 2006 alone the number of registered income taxpayers in South Africa increased from 3.7 million to 4.7 million people.[8] Moreover, the budget deficit (the difference between what the government receives in income and what it spends) fell from 4.5% of GDP in 1994 to a surplus of 1.0% in 2008.[9] Similarly, government debt fell from 43% of GDP in 1994 to 27% in 2009.[10] GDP per capita, in real 2005 rands, increased from just under R29 000 in 1994 to just under R40 000 in 2013.[11] By 2013 almost 6 million net new jobs had been created since 1994.[12]

This economic progress has enabled great improvements in the socio-economic circumstances of South Africa's people. In 1996, 64% of South African households lived in a formal house, 79% had access to piped water, and 47% cooked with electricity. By 2011, some 15 years later, these figures had risen to 70%, 90% and 66% respectively. What these indicators do not adequately convey is the scale of the services delivered. For example, South Africa saw the construction of no fewer than 2,9 million new houses, mostly built by the government or by means of government grants. The number of social welfare beneficiaries increased from about 3.5 million in 2001 to more than 16 million in 2013.[13] That makes the state the biggest single source of income for almost a third of households. By 2012, black households were identifying welfare as almost as important a source of income as employment.[14] The government has therefore been responsible not just for improving the physical circumstances in which people live, but also for an unprecedented injection of cash into the lives of poor people.

As a result the ANC has managed to retain more than 60% of electoral support in all four national elections since 1994, and – until recently, at least – the ruling tripartite alliance (comprising the ANC, COSATU, and the SACP) has also maintained a semblance of political unity. There is general respect for the rule of law (with important exceptions); constitutionally guaranteed institutions such as parliament, the public protector, and the South African Human Rights Commission (SAHRC); and the constitution itself. Considering the nature of the pre-1994 dispensation, these are all achievements worth celebrating.

The ANC has therefore not failed in the main to create a 'better life for all', as it promised in 1994. Any analysis that does not acknowledge this is flawed, and must necessarily fail to explain what is happening in South Africa today, let alone what may happen in the future.

However, it is equally clear that political tensions are mounting, largely due to the difficulty of meeting ever-increasing demands. A cruel irony for the ANC, and the government it leads, is that these improvements are fuelling ever-increasing expectations of further improvements that may not be met since not enough opportunities are being created for citizens, particularly young people, to improve their own lives. The irony is best expressed by the veteran ANC member of parliament and former treason trialist Professor Ben Turok who writes that 'it is consistent with revolutionary theory that people are inspired to struggle when their living standards improve'.[15] This curse of rising expectations lies at the root of much of the social and political instability in the country, and its resolution therefore offers a key to understanding what will happen in the future.

Some negative trends

This curse is exacerbated by the fact that, while much has gone right since 1994, a great deal is also going wrong.

On the economic front, South Africa is unlikely to benefit again from the happy coincidence experienced in the early to mid-2000s of a commodity boom, declining interest rates, low household debt levels, and a weakening rand. Since then, global financial crises have dampened international credit markets, and the domestic household debt-to-income ratio now exceeds 80% – up from 50% in the early 2000s.[16] As a result, consumer spending, which accounts for more than 60% of GDP, is unlikely to boost economic growth to the extent it did in the early to mid-2000s.[17]

Given this, it is questionable whether we will soon reach or exceed the growth levels of about 4% of GDP experienced in 2000-2008. As the Minister of Finance, Pravin Gordhan, pointed out in his medium term budget policy speech on 25 October 2012, growth is likely to average less than 3%

in the short to medium term.[18] Subsequently, a number of economists have suggested that a figure of about 2% may be more realistic.

Slower growth and less tax revenue have resulted in the government running out of the money it needs to implement its policies. South Africa's 2013 budget deficit of 4.8% of GDP was considerably higher than that of other emerging markets such as China, Russia, and Brazil.[19] In 2012, a report by the UN Global Investment Trends Monitor suggested that foreign direct investment in South Africa might have fallen by as much as 43% over the previous 12 months even as it rose in other emerging markets.[20] And, in July 2012, the governor of the Reserve Bank, Gill Marcus, warned that the depreciating currency was becoming a significant inflationary risk.[21] In 2013, after growth forecasts had been downgraded to just 2% of GDP, she again warned that the economic outlook was deteriorating rapidly.[22] Therefore, over the past three to four years, the relatively strong growth, declining debt and deficit levels, and stable inflationary outlook that had characterised the economic environment earlier in the new millennium have all deteriorated.

Furthermore, analysts have increasingly criticised the contradictory nature of economic policy under President Jacob Zuma.[23] For example, the New Growth Path (NGP), developed by the Minister of Economic Development, Ebrahim Patel, envisages a 'state-led growth path' as a strategy for establishing a 'developmental state'.[24] However, the National Development Plan (NDP), developed by the minister responsible for national planning, Trevor Manuel, favours a private sector investment-led growth model, thus contradicting the central thesis of the NGP.[25] Rudolf Gouws, the respected former chief economist of Rand Merchant Bank, now begins some of his briefings on the South African economy with a picture of two angled arrows painted on a road surface, pointing at each other.

Playing with a hand grenade?

The implications of lower levels of GDP growth and investor uncertainty will be felt most acutely in the lives of ordinary people. Despite the government's welfare and service delivery successes, formal levels of unemployment remain extremely high, averaging more than 25%. Among young black people, aged 15 to 24, the figure rises to more than 50%.[26] Only in 2004-2007, when GDP growth averaged more than 5%, did the country experience a sustained decline in the number and proportion of unemployed people.[27]

Taking a measure of relative poverty as an income of about R1500 a month, in 1996 some 40% of South Africans lived in poverty. Sixteen years later, in 2012, that figure had fallen only marginally to 36%.[28] For too many South Africans, the experience of democracy is a life of poverty.

Another major factor is that of inequality, with its well-documented implications for political and social stability. The most commonly used measure of inequality is the Gini coefficient, which ranks the extent of income inequality in a given society on a score between 0 and 1. (A score of 0 would indicate complete equality, with every person in a particular society earning precisely the same amount, and a score of 1 would indicate complete inequality, with one person in the society earning all the income.) In 1996, two years after the democratic transition, South Africa's Gini coefficient was 0.60. By 2012 it had worsened to 0.63,[29] making it one of the most unequal societies in the world.

For these and other reasons, a growing number of analysts and politicians – even leading figures in the ruling party – have sounded alarm bells about persistently high levels of poverty, unemployment and inequality. In June 2012, the Minister of Mineral Resources, Susan Shabangu, appealed to delegates at the South African Mining Lekgotla to do more to address the issue of skills shortage and the 'ticking time-bomb that is the unemployed and unemployable youth of the country's townships and rural streets'.[30] Similarly, in that same year, Zwelinzima Vavi, then general secretary of the Congress of South African Trade Unions (COSATU), told an international policy conference that unemployment, coupled with dehumanising poverty, was a 'ticking time bomb waiting to explode'.[31]

Perhaps most alarmingly, in February 2011 the chairman of the South African Institute of International Affairs (SAIIA), Moeletsi Mbeki, wrote in *Business Day:* 'I can predict when South Africa's "Tunisia Day" will arrive. ... The year will be 2020, give or take a couple of years.' Mbeki was referring to the unexpected and violent North African uprisings that year that led to the collapse of the governments of Tunisia, Egypt, and Libya, and destabilised the entire region. He went on to say that ANC leaders were like a 'group of children playing with a hand grenade. One day, one of them will figure out how to pull out the pin and everyone will be killed.'[32]

In 2012, my colleague John Kane-Berman, then head of the South African Institute of Race Relations, suggested in an address to business and other leaders that the South African political system was approaching a 'tipping point'.[33] Earlier that year I chaired a private dinner where former president FW de Klerk told business and think-tank leaders that South Africa was approaching some kind of tipping point, and could slide very rapidly if some poor policy options currently on the table were exercised.[34]

Even within the ANC there is growing concern: in July 2013 the deputy president, Kgalema Motlanthe, startled observers by warning that, if the ANC failed to remain relevant to the people, it would run the risk of losing power.[35] In that same month the ANC admitted that South Africa's economy risked being left behind, and needed to be urgently reformed. Similarly, in 2013, the former treason trialist and liberation icon Andrew Mlangeni warned that without reform the ANC could lose an election.[36]

These observations and predictions did not appear in a vacuum as there are growing signs of popular dissatisfaction with the government's performance. In the 2009 national elections the ANC won 65.9% of the vote; however, ANC voter support calculated as a proportion of potential voters fell precipitously from 55% in 1994 to just 38% in that 2009 election.[37] Moreover, in that 2009 election, more people chose *not to vote* than to vote for the ANC.

These indicators must be read alongside rising protest action in poor communities. Commonly labelled 'service delivery protests', they are an increasingly prominent feature of post-apartheid South Africa. Often violent, they are triggered by grievances over service delivery and governance, and typically involve mass marches or other mass action, the erection of barricades on public roads, and the destruction of state facilities as well as other property. These protests have escalated significantly in recent years; according to official statistics, crowd management incidents involving unrest (mostly service delivery protests) almost doubled from 622 in 2005/2006 to 1091 in 2011/2012. Between 2009 and 2012 unrest incidents averaged 2.9 per day – an increase of 40% over the 2.1 incidents per day in 2004-2009.[38] In incidents reminiscent of the anti-apartheid struggle, protestors have also torched the houses of local councillors, and some councillors and other local role players have been attacked and killed. Indeed, according to a timeline constructed by Sapa, as many as 50 political figures – many of them local councillors – were killed in the five years prior to 2012.[39]

While the government and ruling party have tended to downplay their significance, the emergence of these protests in a supposedly inclusive constitutional democracy is disconcerting, and analysts are increasingly acknowledging that they are more significant – and more ominous – than the anodyne term 'service delivery protests' suggests. Indeed, Peter Alexander, professor of sociology at the University of Johannesburg, has described them as part of a broader 'rebellion of the poor', which will not subside unless the government becomes far more effective in channelling resources to deprived communities.[40]

Branching off from the high road?

Therefore, despite South Africa's transition to democracy, and the significant improvements in living standards that followed, it is clear that new negative trends and fault lines have also emerged. While they are multifaceted and complex, they all come down to whether our country will be able to meet popular demands for improved standards of living.

This is not a question of whether we have made progress or not. The welfare model, together with free state-led service delivery, has driven great improvements in living standards, but this in turn has heightened expectations of future improvements. However, welfare and free services do not contribute to the growth or investment necessary to finance those future improvements. So, every year, poor communities will expect more and more from government, while it will increasingly struggle to meet those demands.

The key question now is whether these expectations can be met – and, if not, what the social and political consequences are likely to be.

If South Africa cannot meet the demands of its people, and will not have the resources to do so in the foreseeable future, then surely it is at risk of sliding into a dark future. This is the view of veteran role players and commentators such as Moeletsi Mbeki, FW de Klerk and John Kane-Berman. It is the view of international ratings agencies such as Standard and Poor's and Moody's, which in 2012 downgraded South Africa's credit ratings, citing the risk of populist pressure undermining sound fiscal policy.[41] It is also the view of respected international publications such as *The Economist*, which has commented on what it calls South Africa's 'sad decline' while much of the rest of Africa is rising.[42] Even some ANC leaders are acknowledging – in private and even in public – that their time in office may be limited.

Indeed, South Africa's most respected scenario planner, Clem Sunter, has adjusted his own scenarios downwards, saying the odds of the country dropping out of the premier league of nations had increased significantly.[43] His opinion carries a lot of weight as his celebrated 'High Road/Low Road' scenarios of the mid-1980s helped South African decision-makers to identify and understand the 'tipping point' that the country was then rapidly approaching, as well as the vital role their decisions would soon play in setting South Africa off irrevocably on one road or the other.[44] South Africa undoubtedly took the high road, as evidenced by its constitutional settlement and the political, economic, and social recovery outlined above. However, this 'high road' seems to have reached a new crossroads, centred on rising expectations.

The year 2024 – ten years from now – will feature South Africa's seventh inclusive national elections, only three national elections away from today. The world we wake up to the next morning may look very different from the one we inhabit today. Just how different is the question this book sets out to answer.

THE ART OF
TRAVELLING IN TIME

★ ★ ★

The idea that we can describe the world in 2024 suggests that we can travel in time. In this chapter, we explore whether such a feat is at all possible, and, if so, what our time machine should look like, and how it should be piloted.

Academics and other analysts devote much of their time to identifying and explaining changes within countries. These diagnoses mostly deal with the past and the present, and draw on a formidable arsenal of established theory in the process. However, analysts are also often asked to comment on how the countries and economies they study may change in the future. While many try to respond, they often do so hesitantly, and without the benefit of established theories and methods similar to those for dealing with the past and the present. As a result, political scientists have a poor track record of anticipating shifts in political systems.

In fact, many of the most significant political and economic developments during the past 50 years were poorly predicted, or not predicted at all. In 1966, the American scenario planner Gill Ringland recalls, 27 leading American scientists were asked to predict what the world would need and want over the next 20 years.[1] Almost all of the 335 forecasts they generated proved to be entirely incorrect, mostly because they gave too much importance to state-driven megaprojects, which soon began to decline.

In an influential article published in 2003, the scenario planners Peter Kennedy and Charles Thomas (of the Futures Strategy Group in Glastonbury in Connecticut) cited the shock arrivals of the dot-com crisis and 9/11 terror attacks as examples of the failure of conventional political and economic forecasting.[2] Moreover, they warned that a lack of methods for dealing with future uncertainty would lead to more 'future shocks'. Just six years later, and despite all the resources poured into political and economic forecasting, the 2009 global financial crisis took almost everyone by surprise, even though the diagnosis after the fact was relatively straightforward.

Peter Schwartz, former head of the renowned Shell scenario planning team, cites the example of a scenario called 'The Greening of Russia', which Royal Dutch Shell developed in 1983.[3] It held that, should Mikhail Gorbachev rise to power, this could lead to significant political and economic reforms in Russia. However, almost every Soviet expert presented with the scenario said it was entirely implausible. Even the Central Intelligence Agency (CIA) in the United States responded by saying, 'You really don't know what you're talking about.' Of course, in the end Shell was proved right and the CIA forecasters were proved wrong.

More recently the dramatic political events in Tunisia, Egypt, and Libya again took many scholars, diplomats, and journalists by surprise. During subsequent briefings to officials of the United States Department of State in Johannesburg and Washington, I made a point of asking whether the uprisings had been on their long-term political radar, to which the answer was 'no'. I asked the same question during a meeting with representatives of the Israeli government in Jerusalem, and got the same answer.

It is extraordinary that two advanced countries with highly sophisticated intelligence services and enormous interests in the stability of the Middle East and North Africa did not know that the entire region was on the verge of fundamental change. Intelligence agencies, think-tanks and universities in those two countries invest hundreds of millions of dollars a year in research on the Middle East and North Africa, but failed to provide their governments with direct advance warning of these momentous events, which have had far-reaching implications for political and economic stability.

Therefore, both political scientists and economists seem unable to use the standard tools provided by their disciplines to accurately predict the future. As in the case of the collapse of the Soviet Union, the circumstances that gave rise to the North African upheavals were diagnosed in great detail – but only after they had occurred. Crucially, much of this after-the-fact analysis was based on trends that were already in evidence long before the events occurred. This is significant as it suggests that the information necessary to anticipate these upheavals was in fact available but was not adequately identified, analysed and interpreted.

The butterfly effect

Why have attempts to predict major political developments been so singularly unsuccessful? Should political analysts and economists abandon all hope of gaining some insight into the future? Indeed, many economists and political analysts would argue that the future is inherently unpredictable. Thus the scenario planners WK Ralston and Ian Wilson note that mankind's efforts at divining the future, 'from the Delphic oracle, through augury, tarot, and the crystal ball, to the methodologies of the professional forecaster' have all failed to 'penetrate the veil between us and what is to come'.[4]

However, giving up entirely on gaining some insight into the future – and effectively abandoning our futures to fate – would clearly be unsatisfactory. Journalists, business leaders, politicians, military planners, and ordinary people will continue to demand futures insights from economic and political analysts. There is no choice but to persist in studying the futures of political and economic systems, and to try to understand why forecasting methods do not work.

Forecasters concentrate on identifying key current factors and trends and extrapolating them into the future in order to arrive at *a single prediction* or forecast at *a specific point in time*. The problem they run into is the extreme complexity of the current trends and events that will eventually shape the future.

Consider the huge complexity underpinning the political

system in South Africa today. A plethora of actors – including organisations, businesses, political parties, courts of law, diplomats, government departments, newspapers and other media, civil society organisations, and various individuals – are constantly at work trying to change the country – and often in divergent or conflicting ways. It would be impossible to identify each of these participants and gauge the likely impact of their activities in order to understand how and why the country will change in the future.

This was a massive problem I faced when conducting research for a doctoral thesis on scenario planning at North West University (NWU). I sought to develop a method capable of predicting the long-term stability or instability of political and economic systems. However, I soon realised that the extreme complexity of these systems presented a formidable obstacle. My research supervisor, Professor André Duvenhage, and I had many conversations about this, and we eventually concluded that the complexity of political and economic systems was real, and could not be avoided. Seeking to dilute this complexity would therefore result in an artificially simplistic view of reality. By contrast, our work would need to accept the degree of complexity, and then seek to overcome its implications.

We then began to draw heavily on work done in the physical sciences in the first half of the 20th century – an era in which biologists and physicists began to grapple with the extraordinary complexity of the phenomena they were studying. One example cited in a number of academic articles was how biologists became aware of the extreme complexity that underpinned the life of a plant. They realised that it was futile to break the plant down into leaves, stalks, flowers, and roots – and even further to the atomic scale – and study each of these components in isolation, in the hope that they could then reassemble the plant and understand how it could grow. Rather, they began to understand that it was the way in which the plant interacted with its environment – air, sunlight, soil, and water – that explained its life. One could not disaggregate the plant into its component pieces; one had to study it as a whole if one wanted to understand its life and growth. Put differently, the life of a plant was far greater than the sum of its parts.

Another popular example is drawn from physics. The temperature of a gas increases because all the gas molecules rub against one another. In other words, the temperature changes because of the way in which each gas molecule interacts with all the others. Again, it would be futile to try to understand the rise in temperature by studying individual molecules in isolation. All a researcher would then see is a single molecule vibrating in a vacuum.

This work in physics and biology eventually led to the emergence, in the latter half of the 20th century, of what is known as complex systems theory. As its name suggests, it seeks to explain the behaviour of extremely complex systems that, it holds, have the following common characteristics:

- They contain very large numbers of actors or participants.
- Those actors or participants interact regularly with one another.
- Through that interaction they direct feedback into

the system based on how satisfied they are with their circumstances in that system.

There are two types of feedback. The first seeks to stabilise the system and maintain its status quo. This type of feedback is directed by actors or participants who are satisfied with their circumstances. The second seeks to change the system and is directed by actors or participants whose expectations are not being met.

The two types are in constant conflict in any system. Where the former predominates the system will remain stable and will not change. However, where the latter predominates the system will change – and often dramatically.

These interactions and the feedback they produce are emergent, which means that they produce a result that is much greater than the sum of its parts.

This last idea has been popularised as the 'butterfly effect', namely the notion that, when a butterfly flaps its wings on one side of the world, it could cause a storm on the other side.[5]

In my experience, the best example of a complex system, and the one we use most often during our scenario briefings to introduce our audience to complexity theory, is that of traffic in an urban environment. Every day tens of thousands of motor vehicles interact with each other on roads and highways as their drivers make their way to their destinations. We all know that it takes just one actor, such as a broken-down car, or an object lying in the road, to cause a stoppage or slowdown, which rapidly builds up into a traffic jam, and eventually into a total system failure known as 'gridlock'. The knock-on effects are enormous, ranging from the human and material costs of accidents to huge sums in lost economic productivity. It would be futile to study each vehicle in a traffic jam to understand its cause. A traffic jam can only be explained by examining how the vehicles in question interacted with one another. Therefore, major traffic jams and their consequences are a perfect example of the emergent property of complex systems – or the butterfly effect at work.

At North West University, we developed the proposition that similar effects can be observed in any political or economic system. A small and seemingly insignificant change in the behaviour of just one actor in such a system can affect all the other actors in that system, and eventually change its future. We produced the following very simple equations to demonstrate this effect as it might play itself out in a political system:

Imagine that there are only three actors, or participants, in the South African economy, and assume that each contributes a value of 2 to the economy. If the economy was a simple system, in which participants made these contributions in isolation of one another, the system could be expressed by adding their contributions together, as follows:

$$2 + 2 + 2 = 6$$

However, in the case of a more complex system, the individual contributions or components would need to be multiplied, as follows:

$$2 \times 2 \times 2 = 8$$

Now consider what happens if at some point in the future one of the actors contributes a 1 and not a 2 to the system. The simple system would now look like this:

$$2 + 2 + 1 = 5$$

Here the outcome for the system has changed from a value of 6 to a 5. Had a forecast been made of the future of such a system, and the forecaster had been unaware that one of the actors in the system would no longer contribute a 2 to the system, the forecast would still have been reasonably accurate. However, the complex system would change radically, as follows:

$$2 \times 2 \times 1 = 4$$

Here, the outcome for the system has changed from an 8 to a 4. This time, had a forecast been made of the future of this system, and the forecaster been unaware that one of the actors would no longer contribute a 2, the forecast would have been totally wrong.

These calculations are perfect illustrations of the butterfly effect – in other words, that a small, seemingly inconsequential, change in the behaviour of even one actor in a system of millions of actors could dramatically change the future of that system. This is why no one can forecast what the traffic will be like at any given point in the future. The fact that the actions of just one vehicle or driver can completely thwart the plans of all other drivers makes such a forecast impossible.

John Kane-Berman is fond of telling a story about the

former National Party and later Herstigte Nasionale Party politician Jaap Marais that effectively demonstrates the quality of emergence, or the butterfly effect, in a political context. In 1968 the then prime minister, John Vorster, agreed that the Springboks could play an All Black team that included Maoris. Marais warned him that such a compromise would one day cause 'a black man to marry your daughter, and sit next to you in parliament'. His NP colleagues laughed this off, but Marais was actually right: in compromising once on the principle of racial separation, Vorster unintentionally contributed to a chain of events that would culminate in the ending of apartheid.

No forecaster could possibly have realised what the consequences of Vorster's decision would be. Consider the thousands of significant decisions taken every year over the life of the apartheid system by a huge range of role players including the NP government, political movements in exile, internal resistance movements, civil society organisations, foreign governments and other international institutions, and many others, and one starts to realise why accurately predicting the future at that point was effectively impossible.

What our research at NWU revealed is that, in the case of complex systems such as political systems, the future can never be accurately forecast to a single point in time and space. Such forecasts are largely based on known trends, which are then projected into the future,[6] but even a seemingly insignificant shift in one of those trends can completely change its future trajectory.

We concluded that all the past failures of political and economic forecasting resulted from this problem.[7] It is not possible for any analyst, no matter how well-informed, to track every single shift in South Africa's current political system – and therefore equally impossible for any forecaster to extrapolate current trends into a single accurate prediction of the future. For this reason we need to do what many scenario thinkers have done before, and that is to move away from the idea that a single pre-ordained future exists and rather reassess our view of the future and how we think about it.

Four types of futures

In his excellent book *20/20 Foresight: Crafting Strategy in an Uncertain World*, the futurist Hugh Courtney comes up with the radical and brilliant idea that there are different variants or types of futures that are distinguished from one another by their relative uncertainty. He cites four such types, namely:

- A '**clear enough future**', when the range of possible outcomes is so narrow that uncertainty does not matter. This does not imply that such a future is perfectly predictable, but rather that it is predictable enough for a dominant strategy of choice to suit all plausible outcomes.
- An '**alternate future**', when it is possible to identify a limited set of possible outcomes. In this instance, Courtney cites potential legislative or judicial changes as examples.
- A '**range of futures**', when the future is more uncertain

than an 'alternate future', as it is not possible to identify a shortlist of *possible* outcomes. Rather, it is necessary to develop a broad range of *plausible* outcomes. Courtney cites unstable macro-economic conditions as an example of such a future.

- A **'truly ambiguous future'**, when it may be difficult even to identify a range of possible outcomes. The impact of major economic or social discontinuities is an example of this kind of future.[8]

Courtney's analysis is of great value since it shows us that there is not just one kind of future that applies to all economies and all countries. Instead, we should rather categorise the different variants or kinds of futures according to their relative uncertainty. This will help us navigate these futures. Most importantly, and this really is something to get your head around, in very uncertain environments a number of different futures may be possible for the same country.

While Courtney notes that some types of futures are more uncertain than others, Ralston and Wilson warn that the future of most systems is becoming increasingly uncertain all the time. This, they argue, is due to the concept of 'change in the character of change itself' – another idea that requires some thinking. Here they cite the growing number of people working to change the world, especially in areas of technological innovation, and the 'radical compression' of the time taken for these innovations to be developed. They assert that innovations in areas of information technology, nuclear power, biomedical advances, and nanotechnology 'will have a more pervasive influence on human life than any other previous technologies in human history'.[9]

Hence futures researchers need to be aware not only that some futures are more uncertain than others, but also that many futures are becoming increasingly uncertain all the time. Which type or variant of the future is most relevant to a particular analyst will therefore depend on what aspect of a system is being studied, and within what time frame this is being done.

For example, if a corporation commissioned us to determine whether the ANC would still be in power after the 2014 elections, this would suggest a 'clear enough' or 'alternate' future, as a range of possible outcomes could be listed. These would include the ANC losing the election, being driven from power by popular protests, being eroded by internal conflict, and so on. The point is that it would be possible to list a short number of possible outcomes, and to be sure that one of these will come to pass.

However, as time frames lengthen, the emergent character (or butterfly effect) of South Africa's political system will probably mean that the type of future will become the third or even the fourth variant where we would have to suggest a number of different plausible outcomes for the country and not just a single forecast of a single future.

The advent of scenario planning

There is, of course, a considerable difference between predicting a single future and developing a series of plausible ones. As I have shown, the method of forecasting – in seeking to identify a single most probable outcome – is a risky method for determining South Africa's political future. The uncertainty inherent in the butterfly effect is simply too great for such a forecast to succeed other than by sheer luck.

Yet many institutions and other role players still demand or expect these sorts of forecasts. The continued use of this approach explains why political scientists and economists struggle to accurately predict the future of economies and countries. It therefore appears that a more effective method is required if we are to understand what South Africa's future holds.

Pierre Wack, perhaps the world's most respected scenario planner, and the forefather of much current futures research, made exactly this point almost 30 years ago when he wrote that, despite the obvious failures of forecasting, many corporations continue to do so 'because no one has developed a better way of dealing with economic uncertainty'.[10] According to Wack the answer to poor forecasting is not to hire better forecasters. He argued that the future is too uncertain for any forecasting technique to be effective, and that it is necessary to develop new and better methods – namely scenario methods – for studying the future.

There is a fascinating history behind the scenario methods Wack was referring to, and understanding this history is essential to understanding exactly why these methods are so effective. A number of great books have been written on the subject but what follows is an abridged history.

The methodology of scenario planning developed in response to the great uncertainties presented by the advent of the Cold War when two superpowers – the Soviet Union and the United States – confronted each other in a binary nuclear standoff. Strategic planning failures in such an environment could obviously have had catastrophic consequences. Just think of the implications of either party developing an entirely inaccurate perception of the other's intentions, while both have their finger on the nuclear button.

In this tense environment, the Rand Corporation was established in order to conduct research into new weapons systems, particularly for the United States Air Force.[11] A researcher at the Rand Corporation, Hermann Kahn, developed a new method for gaining insight into the future by developing descriptions of a series of alternative futures – written in the present tense, as if they had already come to pass.[12] He called them 'scenarios', the movie term for a detailed screenplay.[13] The Californian thrash metal band Megadeth takes its name from one of these scenarios, which describes how one million lives are lost in a nuclear blast.[14]

Kahn went on to found the Hudson Institute in the 1960s, which produced a number of Cold War scenarios, centred on alternative accounts of nuclear conflict.[15] The Hudson Institute began to attract sponsorship from large corporations such as General Motors, IBM, and Royal Dutch Shell,[16] which led to them being exposed to early scenario thinking. General Electric, for example, decided to include scenarios in its approach to strategic planning.

However, the role and status of scenario development as a tool for gaining greater insight into the future was only consolidated by a series of events that started in the planning department of Royal Dutch Shell in 1967, and culminated in the 1973 Yom Kippur War. By the mid-1960s, Royal Dutch Shell had realised that extreme long-term planning – beyond that provided by traditional planning and forecasting methods – was necessary in the oil industry. [17] As a result, it began to look ahead to the likely business environment in the year 2000.[18] According to Wack[19] – who led Shell's planning efforts – and Gill Ringland,[20] this study indicated that 'the predictable, surprise-free [oil industry] environment would not continue', and identified the possibility of a major shift in the balance of power between oil companies and oil producers in favour of the latter that would significantly increase the price of oil. At the same time the Organization of Petroleum Exporting Countries (OPEC) had begun to '[flex] its political muscles'.[21]

The conclusions of the Shell study were significant, as both oil prices and supply had seemed predictable since the mid-1940s.[22] In response to this newly identified uncertainty, Shell broke with traditional forecasting practice and produced two detailed scenarios of the global oil system.[23] One suggested that the oil price would remain stable, which was the globally accepted opinion at that time. The other suggested that the oil price would rise significantly. Shell realised that the Arab oil-producing countries could and would demand higher oil prices. The question that could not be answered was when this would happen.[24]

The oil industry is obviously a complex system. Scores of producer nations supply scores of consumer nations, who in turn supply billions of oil users and hundreds and thousands of businesses that depend directly and indirectly on the supply and price of oil. In the event, the impetus for the increase in the oil price was provided in 1973 by the Yom Kippur War between Israel and its Middle Eastern neighbours.[25] Arab nations resented Western support for Israel. Within weeks, ordinary motorists around the world faced steeply rising petrol prices.

This changed the balance of power between mainly Western oil companies and their mainly Middle Eastern suppliers just as Shell had suggested (and its directors had been alone in planning for).[26] This could not have been achieved through traditional methods of forecasting. As a result, it was better placed than other global oil companies to respond to the price increases, which allowed it to assume a leading role in the global oil business.[27]

Following the shock of events round the Yom Kippur War, and growing awareness of Shell's pioneering approach, a significant number of Fortune 100 companies went on to adopt scenario-based planning.[28] A survey of 200 large corporations soon identified scenario-based planning as the most common strategic planning tool.[29]

A growing appreciation of the potential consequences of strategic errors in the Cold War context therefore forced some analysts to adopt a new approach to studying the future. This method caused them to dispense with the notion that there was one pre-ordained future, and that capable forecasters could accurately identify that future. Instead, they abandoned the certainty promised by traditional forecasting methods in favour of identifying a range of equally plausible futures for the same system or country. This is what later enabled Shell's scenario planners to identify the possibility that Gorbachev could bring about major political and economic reforms in Russia.

Professor Duvenhage and I immediately understood that the strength, and later success, of this method could be ascribed to a single characteristic, namely its inherent ability to overcome the butterfly effect. For this reason scenario planning dovetailed very neatly with our work on complex systems and freed us from guessing at the future. In scenario planning we therefore found a methodology we could apply to our work on complex systems theory to determine the prospects for South Africa's long-term stability. The final conclusions of that study are the focus of this book.

The failure of analysts and economists to anticipate events such as the Arab Spring and the global financial crisis therefore suggests two things. The first is that the butterfly effect means that the future of complex systems is plural rather than singular. The second is that scenario building is the only method that can overcome the consequences of the butterfly effect.

Therefore, in the case of South Africa, any serious attempt to gain greater insight into our future must be based on a series of equally plausible scenarios, plus – and this will become very important in this book – a method for navigating our way through time towards the scenario that will eventually materialise.

TEN STEPS TO BUILDING SCENARIOS

A number of scenario planners have written that scenarios are very powerful instruments in that they provide their users with a sense of standing in the future and looking back at the present. When they are well written, this sensation is so intense that it often persuades people to change their current behaviour to avoid unfavourable futures, and to realise more favourable ones. For that reason, often the point of developing and disseminating scenarios is to change the present behaviour of governments, as well as business and political leaders.

What are scenarios really? How are they built, and what are they meant to accomplish? Scenario theorists and planners often use analogies to illuminate the nature and function of scenarios, and it is useful to start by recounting some of these.

My friend and colleague Louis van der Merwe of the Centre for Innovative Leadership, a South African scenario consultancy, uses a brilliant illustration involving the weather.

According to him, most people probably have some confidence in weather forecasts for the following day. If the forecaster says it will rain, many will take umbrellas to work, and, if the forecaster says it will be cold, they will dress warmly. A smaller number of people will have the same degree of confidence in a two-day weather forecast, and an even smaller number in a three-day, four-day or five-day forecast. Eventually all people will reach their 'predictable horizon' – the point at which they begin to lose confidence in the accuracy of a given forecast. The level of uncertainty around forecasts grows as they are projected further and further into the future.

In this context, consider a family leaving on a ten-day holiday. Among other things, they pack an umbrella, and perhaps some warm clothes. They do not do this because of a weather forecast – ten days into the future is too far beyond their predictable horizon. The items are not packed because they know it will rain, or even because they think it might rain. Rather, the family knows it could be hot or cold, wet or dry, and therefore they weigh up which combination of these factors is most plausible. They then decide to take an umbrella because it could rain, and some warm clothes, because it could be cold. Unwittingly, this family has done some scenario planning.

Weather scenarios are relatively straightforward because the weather can only be hot, cold, wet or dry, or a combination of these factors. Scenarios involving South Africa's political future are infinitely more complex because a myriad of social, economic, and political factors are at play. However, the principles applied by the family going on holiday remain valid, and it remains a good example. It also illustrates the difference between scenario planning and forecasting, as practised by the weather forecasters on the evening news.

The evening weather forecast is an exercise in predicting a single future at a single point in time. However, as we noted in the previous chapter, the butterfly effect means that the future of any complex system is in fact plural and this explains why economists and political analysts often struggle to accurately predict future trends.

Ringland compares scenario planning to wind tunnels.[1] Wind tunnels seek to anticipate the real-world behaviour of aircraft and motor vehicles, among others. Just as a wind tunnel allows an aircraft designer to establish the likely future behaviour of his or her aircraft, scenario planning allows analysts to anticipate how the systems they study may behave in the future. Just as the aircraft designers can suspend their model aircraft in a wind tunnel to see how they react to certain air flows, long before they will actually be built, we can hang our political or economic systems in a metaphorical wind tunnel and expose them to different sets of variables to see how they will fly.

The weather and wind tunnel analogies reveal that scenario planning is very different from forecasting. Three such differences are commonly identified by scenario planners and they represent the principles upon which most scenario-planning methods rest.

The first is that scenarios are not forecasts or predictions of what will happen in the future.[2] Forecasters predict a single state at a single point in the future, which they argue will come to pass. By contrast, scenarios describe a set or series of alternative futures, all of which are more or less equally plausible.[3]

Second, forecasts often vary around a 'midpoint base case'.[4] This means they tend to vary around a single common theme, such as what the ANC government may or may not do with respect to South Africa's economic policy. By contrast, scenarios take account of a far broader range of variables. For instance, a well-developed set of scenarios would not just consider the future of economic policy under the ANC but also force analysts to think about what could happen with economic policy should the ANC no longer be around. In this way, scenarios expose analysts and end users to a broader range of variables, and reduce their vulnerability to unexpected external events.

Third, forecasts are typically 'snapshots' of the future at a single point in time.[5] By contrast, scenarios draw pathways from the present to several different outcomes, thus providing analysts with the advantage of considering a full series of events between the present and the future.

Scenarios and forecasts therefore find themselves at the opposite ends of the spectrum of methods for studying the future. To rely on forecasting means that you will be left with only one possible future to consider. If that future does not materialise, you will have no other plan or strategy to fall back on. When applied to a complex system, such as South Africa's economy, a forecast therefore creates a misleading sense of accuracy and simplicity. By contrast, if you rely on scenario planning you will have several plausible futures to consider – which is consistent with the implications of the butterfly effect.

The desire for certainty

If scenarios are not forecasts or predictions, and produce a series of equally plausible futures instead of a single one, this raises obvious questions about their utility. How, for example, must an investor decide on whether to build a multi-million dollar plant in a country that may or may not be unstable in ten years' time? Surely, only a concrete forecast could help a board of directors take such key long-term strategic decisions.

One response is that, due to the butterfly effect, long-term predictions of the futures of complex systems are bound to be incorrect in any case. This is because those futures still need to evolve over a certain period, during which time relatively small changes in present circumstances, or relatively small actions by any one of a wide range of actors, may cause significant changes.

A second response, cited by a number of scenario planners, is that, since scenarios are not forecasts, their utility does not hinge on whether any of them will turn out to be entirely accurate. Rather, by developing a series of plausible futures, and spelling out the pathways from the present to those futures, they present scenario planners and strategists with a series of route maps to the future. By studying unfolding events at any point ahead of the scenario horizon, users of a scenario can gain a sense of which scenario they are moving towards and adjust their planning and strategy accordingly.

Despite this, the craving for certainty still tempts some planners to reject the scenario approach in favour of forecasting. Many governments and businesses still want, and demand, a higher level of certainty than that offered by scenario planning. I know from my own work that this is true of many South

African companies. It is very frustrating to see companies that have been burned over and over again by failed forecasts persisting with this method because they crave the simplicity and certainty promised by a single future. Many South African companies and other institutions routinely develop inaccurate forecasts of GDP growth and inflation, and then have to revise them over and over again. They could escape from this cycle if they understood that the forecasts will probably never be accurate – no matter how good the forecasters are.

For example, in 2005 a prominent group of economists forecast that South African GDP growth would average 4%-5% over the next five years. Due to the global financial crisis – a typical unforeseen event – GDP growth averaged less than 3% over this period, and even contracted by 2% in 2009. These economists are among the best in the country, and among the best in the world. The reason they were wrong is that they were trying to produce a single forecast for a very complex system.

Despite this, the desire for certainty persists. Consider my discussion with a strategic planner for a major furniture chain. He agreed with me that forecasting was futile, but said his board demanded one future, and he had been tasked with producing it. However, by reverting to the familiar and seemingly clear option of a single forecast, his board exposed itself to the consequences of the butterfly effect, and hence the danger of basing their business operations on a misleading picture of the future. Therefore, while the craving to gain certainty about the future is both understandable and tempting, it should be resisted when dealing with complex systems. Moreover, scenario consultants Ralston and Wilson warn that the growing uncertainty of global and regional environments is leading to a 'corresponding decrease in the accuracy and utility of forecasting.'[6]

Probably the most powerful argument against forecasting is provided by Pierre Wack of Shell fame. He argued that forecasts are only accurate when known trends change very slowly. When the trends underpinning a given forecast change more rapidly, or are actually broken, the forecast necessarily fails. However, this is precisely the moment at which an accurate forecast would have been most useful.[7]

Again, a good example is that of the recent political upheavals in Egypt, Libya, and other parts of the Middle East and North Africa. Conventional forecasts continued to project a stable region, based on trends that pointed to well-entrenched regimes. When young people in those countries turned on their leaders, and overthrew them in the case of Egypt and Libya, it took the whole world by surprise. In exactly the same way that many oil companies in the 1970s were unprepared for the oil price shock, many governments and corporations were entirely unprepared for the rapid power shifts in North Africa and the Middle East.

In political science, no single university department or think-tank can claim that it had forecast both the nature and timing of recent events in these regions. The fundamental reason for this is that these events simply could not be forecast. Egypt today differs so greatly from Egypt 20 years ago that a single-point forecast of the overthrow of the Mubarak regime would not have been possible. However, a well-developed series of scenarios might well have anticipated growing youth dissent and a resultant major power shift in the region.

The same is true of South Africa. The trend of the ANC winning one election after the other with more than 60% of the vote is firmly established. When the Centre for Risk Analysis (CRA) first started producing scenarios in which the ANC had lost power, many people laughed. A professor of politics at a prominent South African university suggested that we did not understand how the world worked. Jacob Zuma, too, is fond of saying that his party will govern until the Second Coming. Well, just imagine what it must have been like for diplomats in North Africa and the Middle East to have to phone their foreign desks in Washington and London and explain that there seemed to be a revolution on the go. Within a year, the governments of Tunisia, Libya, and Egypt had collapsed. Or think how ridiculous it would have been to declare after PW Botha's Rubicon speech in 1985 that within 20 years the last leader of the NP would be an ANC cabinet minister.

In South Africa's case, growing service delivery protests may lead some forecasters to argue that by 2024 the ANC will have been overthrown. More and more people may agree with this view, given persistent inequality together with the growing infighting in the ANC and the ruling alliance. Therefore, should a planner reject scenarios in favour of forecasting, this is a forecast he may make. The problem, of course, is that the ANC may respond by introducing reforms that boost GDP growth, employment, and incomes. Ten years into the future, South Africa could be an increasingly prosperous middle-income economy led by an even stronger ANC.

If a company had chosen not to invest in South Africa

based on the flawed forecast, it would have lost an opportunity to make a lot of money. That is the price it would have paid for the certainty it had sought. However, if it had been allowed to consider a range of plausible scenarios, it could have made an informed risk-versus-reward decision about building a new factory in South Africa.

Neither method would have provided it with complete certainty, but the forecast could easily have turned out to be entirely wrong, whereas the scenarios would have provided it with a broader choice around a limited number of options – and a vital route map of how to get to the future.

Take the example of the South African mining industry, which is currently in the doldrums, and faces the double onslaught of increasingly hostile government policy and trade union militancy. It is no secret that the extent of this onslaught has caught many in the industry by surprise. This could have been avoided if the industry had put a number of serious mining scenarios together some ten years ago. These would almost certainly have revealed the adverse circumstances South African mining companies confront today, and allowed them to plan accordingly.

Ten steps to building effective scenarios

Adopting a scenario approach to gain strategic insight into the future of a country or an economy therefore has significant advantages over a forecasting approach. So how would one go about building such a set of scenarios? When applied to a country's political or economic future, as in our case, this process should follow the following ten steps:[8]

★ ★ ★ **STEP 1** ★ ★ ★
Decide what you want to achieve

The first step in any scenario building exercise is to decide exactly what one wants to achieve. Our aim is to establish what it will be like to live in South Africa in 2024. Will there still be good schools? Will property rights still be respected? Will our children find jobs, and be able to study at good universities? Or will conditions have deteriorated? Will the poor have risen up in a second revolution? Will a racist government rule with impunity? Will South Africans with the means to do so look for ways of escaping, and start a new life abroad?

★ ★ ★ **STEP 2** ★ ★ ★
Determine the level of contentment with the status quo

The second step is to establish if citizens want to change the status quo in the country in question or whether they are satisfied with their circumstances in the society being studied. A thorough understanding of the current political, economic, and social environment should be developed. We need to establish who is participating in those environments, and what their expectations are. Are they rich or poor? Content or desperate? And, if so, to what extent?

Again, in our case, this will involve describing what is actually going on in South Africa today. We need to know how the economy is performing, and whether it can deliver the growth, jobs, and wealth to satisfy public expectations. Do we really have the worst education system in the world? What are the current levels of corruption in the public and private sectors? Are they worsening or improving? How angry are the young and unemployed really?

★ ★ ★ STEP 3 ★ ★ ★
Establish whether major political and economic role players are able to change the future

The third step is to understand whether major actors or role players in the country (such as political parties, business, civil society, the youth, and the media) have the means to change the future. Is the society in question a free and open one that can easily be changed by means of lobbying, political activism, and electoral processes? Or is it a closed and undemocratic political system that can only be changed through violent revolution?

In our case, this will depend on whether the rule of law is maintained, property rights are respected, the courts remain independent, the media is free, civil society is allowed to operate, and free political activity is allowed. The alternative would be that all these democratic institutions are eroded by an increasingly powerful state until South Africans lose all control over their future and the government can rule with impunity.

★ ★ ★ STEP 4 ★ ★ ★
Analyse the policy environment

The fourth step is to gain a thorough understanding of the policy environment in the country or economy being studied.

What are the major current policies? How successful are they? If they are not successful, why have they been adopted? If the government is under pressure, does it have room to move on policy, and in what direction?

In our case, the question is: Does the government have a vision or national plan, and can it work? Much has been written about the National Development Plan (NDP) that the cabinet recently adopted as South Africa's developmental blueprint for the next 20 years. However, some analysts say the plan is an exercise in smoke and mirrors, and that the government has no real long-term vision for South Africa, or the political will to implement that vision.

★ ★ ★ **STEP 5** ★ ★ ★
Develop a structured list of trends

The fifth step is to take all the information produced by steps 2, 3, and 4 and to set them out in a structured list of trends. Initially this will result in a huge amount of often contradictory and seemingly confusing information. However, as one begins to sort and organise the information, some clear trends – between, say, 30 and 50 – will begin to emerge.

★ ★ ★ **STEP 6** ★ ★ ★
Identify highways to the future

The sixth step then is to identify a number of major trends that will play a key role in determining the future direction of the country or system in question. Peter Schwartz, who succeeded

Pierre Wack at Shell, and other scenario planners describe these as 'key driving forces'. These trends are so powerful that, depending on how they play out, they have the capacity to change the future of any given system or country.

While this should not be artificially limited in one way or another, some five to ten of these trends can usually be identified. These trends or key driving forces can lead us to diverse extremes. The direction economic policy takes is a typical example of such a trend – with nationalisation on the one extreme and private ownership of the economy on the other. In this sense these trends provide us with highways that we can use to help navigate our way into the future.

★ ★ ★ **STEP 7** ★ ★ ★
Identify road signs and route markers

The seventh step is to identify important road signs and route markers along these highways to the future. These will show that we should turn one way or the other in order to reach a certain destination. U-turns are also possible, should the government start to run out of road in a specific direction. There will also be warning signs and even stop signs, where the economy runs out of steam. These road signs and route markers will provide us with much of the information we need to navigate our way into the future.

At the same time, we should bear in mind that trends do not act in isolation of one another. Rather, complex systems theory dictates that these trends, and the actors driving them, constantly interact with each other to produce results far greater than the sum of their parts. If one wants to use the scenario method, it is vital to understand how these trends interact, and what the results of that interaction may be.

★ ★ ★ **STEP 8** ★ ★ ★

Rank trends by impact and uncertainty

To start understanding this interaction, one has to rank the major trends in terms of two criteria: their potential impact on the system and the degree of uncertainty about what their impact will be. For example, no one I deal with has a sure sense of where current economic policy is headed. It would therefore rank as a very uncertain trend.

This ranking is often done on a graph with two axes: one indicating the degree of impact, and the other the degree of uncertainty. All the major trends are then placed somewhere on this graph, varying between four extremes: high impact and high uncertainty; low impact and high uncertainty; high impact and low uncertainty; and low impact and low uncertainty; as suggested by the graph below:

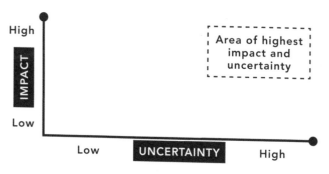

Impact and uncertainty of major trends

★ ★ ★ STEP 9 ★ ★ ★
Produce a matrix

The ninth step is to produce a matrix based on the two most important and most uncertain trends identified in the impact/uncertainty graph on the previous page. These two trends then become the axes of a matrix, and the scenarios are developed in the quadrants formed by these axes. For example, if economic growth and political stability are identified as the two most important and uncertain trends influencing the future of a system, the matrix would be constructed with these two trends as its axes as on the figure below.

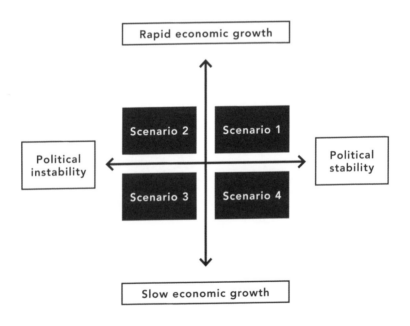

A scenario matrix

Scenario 1 would describe a society shaped by high levels of economic growth in a stable political environment. Scenario 2 would describe a society shaped by high levels of economic growth in an environment of growing political instability. Scenario 3 would describe a society shaped by low levels of economic growth in an unstable political environment. Finally, scenario 4 would describe a society shaped by low levels of economic growth, but in a stable political environment.

It is important to state here that the selection of two trends to form these axes does not mean that the others have been discarded. They will all be reincorporated or reconsidered in the final step outlined below.

★ ★ ★ STEP 10 ★ ★ ★
Write the scenarios

The tenth and final step is to write out the final scenarios. The scenarios in the four quadrants of the scenario matrix are outlines, or wire frames, of four possible futures, based on the interplay of the two most important and most uncertain trends.

In order to turn these outlines into fully fledged scenarios, we now need to flesh them out by adding the impacts of all the other trend highways identified in step 6, as well as some of the road signs and route markers identified in step 7, until this particular future comes alive and forms a coherent whole. In Schwartz's terminology, each key driving force must be incorporated into each scenario framework, and the practitioner must now 'weave the pieces together to form a narrative',[9] comprising a description of a certain future.

The idea here is to suspend disbelief, imagine that you are standing in each of these broad futures, and create a fleshed-out version of this future, taking into account all the other trends, as well as how this future developed over time, emphasising vital points of divergence with the other futures. This is similar to describing Nelson Mandela's inauguration as president on the day it occurred by recounting the train of events that brought the country to this point since PW Botha's Rubicon speech in 1985. The only difference is that you would be writing this description the morning after the Rubicon speech – a decade before Mandela was inaugurated.

To an extent, one is engaging in some kind of research-based time travel – hence the title of this book. When this is done effectively, it gives readers an almost magical sense of standing in that future and looking back at the present, with the highways behind them, and the road signs and markers showing them how they got here over time.

Given this, we now need to get started with the actual scenario building process and determine whether South Africans are content with the status quo or whether there is growing demand for radical economic, social and political change. Should we uncover that South Africans are not satisfied with the current situation, we have to ask, what, if anything, they can do to bring about fundamental change in the country.

ARE WE HEADING FOR A SECOND REVOLUTION?

★ ★ ★

In this book we will be doing some time travelling and trying to establish what it will be like to live in South Africa in 2024. To do this we need to determine the level of satisfaction among South Africans with the status quo – are they happy with the present economic, political and social situation? If not, we then need to ask a second question, which is whether they have the capacity to turn things around.

These are the two most important questions one can ask about the future of any country: Do its citizens want it to be run in a fundamentally different way? Do they have the means to bring a new dispensation about? If the answers to both questions are yes we can anticipate that a considerable degree of change could be lurking, just out of sight, over the South African horizon.

In chapter 2, we showed how a complex system comprises a myriad of actors who compete with each other for resources and how this causes them to direct different types of feedback into the system. One type of feedback would seek to stabilise the system and maintain the status quo – this would result from citizens satisfied with their experience of the system. The other type – directed at changing the country – would result from those who are angry and dissatisfied. Complex systems theory dictates that, when the latter type of feedback exceeds the former, the country or region in question must change – and often dramatically so, as we saw in North Africa.

In the case of the North African uprisings, the answer to the first question was yes; people were tired of living under corrupt dictators and they wanted their circumstances to change. The answer to the second question was ultimately also yes, in that people were able to launch revolutions and overthrow those dictators. The fact that the uprisings took so many analysts by surprise shows that they were not asking the right questions, and, even if some did, they were not getting the right answers.

Even the most cursory examination of the current economic, social, and political environment suggests that in South Africa's case the answer to the first question would also be yes – South Africans are not satisfied with the status quo and they want the country they live in to change.

The economic environment

Probably the most important benchmark of citizens' happiness or satisfaction is the extent to which they are able to participate in the economy and pursue their hopes and dreams. Yet, in South Africa few people are participating in the economy through employment. In 2013 the unemployment rate was 26% – which is far worse than the average rate for South Africa's partners in the BRICS alliance, respectively Brazil (6%), Russia (8%), India (11%), and China (6%).[1]

More importantly, in 2013, the labour market participation rate, or the proportion of people of working age who were either employed or actively looking for work, was just 50% for women and 62% for men.[2] A few years before, the combined male and female participation rate for Argentina (data for Brazil is not available), China, India, and Russia was 78%, 82%, 83%, and 75% respectively.

Largely due to our unemployment rates, huge inequalities exist among South Africans. In 2012, for example, black people received 13 cents in income for every rand earned by their white compatriots – a figure on a par with that in 1994.[3] In 2012, only 1.4 million (or less than 10%) of South Africa's 14.7 million households spent more than R10 000 a month, while more than 7 million (or just under 50%) spent less than R1 799 a month.[4] It is therefore not surprising that South Africa's Gini coefficient is one of the highest in the world. In 2009 (the most recent year for which the World Bank has comparable data) it was 0.631, which compared very badly with the Gini coefficients of Brazil (0.547), Russia (0.401), India (0.334), and China (0.425) respectively.[5]

Consequently, the economic environment features large numbers of very poor people. If poverty is defined as per capita income of less than R1 450 a month, 36% of South Africans were poor in 2012, virtually unchanged from 40.6% in 1996. While the figure for blacks was 42%, the figure for whites was only 0.8%.[6] As a result of these inequalities, very few citizens are taxpayers – in 2013, there were effectively only 6 million individual taxpayers[7] out of a total population of 49.5 million, which includes 32.3 million adults and 13.1 million employed people.[8] Put differently, there was only one taxpayer for every five adults and every two employed people.

In the most general sense you can think of our economic environment as being occupied by two groups. The first are the unemployed and the poor, including the 50% of households who spend less that R1 799 a month. Then there is the *relatively* wealthy – those who spend more than R10 000 per month and the 20% of adults who pay income tax. Just think about it: simply by spending R10 000 per month or by paying income tax you qualify as a member of South Africa's economic elite. Both the relatively wealthy and the poor are important role players but in light of their great majority the poor have an extraordinarily powerful hold over South Africa's future.

Much smaller in number than the poor and the unemployed, but arguably as influential, are national and international investors, whose decisions greatly influence the economy and the prosperity of the country. It is therefore cause for concern that many of these actors regard the investment climate as uncertain, and even adverse. For example, South Africa's ranking as a mining investment destination only came in at 64th out of 96 countries in 2013 despite our wealth of minerals and resources and our world-beating mining engineers.[9] In October 2011, Mark Cutifani, then CEO of AngloGold Ashanti, warned that mining companies were delaying capital investments in South Africa as a result of uncertainty around nationalisation.[10]

Mining industry leaders were not the only major economic role players who were expressing concern about the investment environment. In July 2011 the former governor of the Reserve Bank Tito Mboweni asserted that 'reckless' economic policy debates within the ANC were deterring investment.[11] In November 2010, the chairman of the Gauteng Law Council, Advocate Johann Scholtz, cautioned that poorly functioning courts were forcing investors to resort to arbitration processes to settle disputes.[12] In June 2011 the minister responsible for national planning, Trevor Manuel, declared that the failing education system was hampering economic progress.[13] This is not a recent concern. In 2001, for example, the Production Management Institute warned that the poor quality output of the school system could cause business to 'grind to a halt'.[14]

Even leading figures in the government and the ruling party have been voicing their concerns in public. As early as 25 November 2005, the then deputy president, Phumzile Mlambo-Ngcuka, warned that the 'cost and complexity of regulatory compliance' was becoming an obstacle to investment.[15] In July 2013 the secretary general of the ANC, Gwede Mantashe, warned that South Africa was being left behind by its emerging market peers. Later that month, he declared that Zanu-PF had 'destroyed' the Zimbabwean economy, and added that South Africa could not afford to go down the same road.

Deteriorating investor sentiment is clearly visible in South Africa's investment data. For example, between 2006 and 2012 private business investment in South Africa started to flatten out and averaged roughly between R220 billion and R250 billion per year over that period – after having grown quite quickly over the previous decade. Over the same period (2006-2012) government investment into South Africa – financed by taxes and borrowing (and now e-tolls) – increased by almost 100%.[16] The reason for this is that private investors are afraid of committing capital to South Africa's economy since they do not trust its policy-makers – often with good reason.

The same trend is evident in terms of foreign investment. Between 2008 and 2012 foreign investors' contribution to fixed investment (for instance in factories and new mines) in South Africa declined from 14.3% to just 6.1%.[17] Consequently, the South African economy has grown far more slowly than the economies of its emerging market peers. In the period 1994 to 2013, the South African economy averaged growth of around 3% of GDP – half the average rate recorded by the other BRICS countries.

Despite extensive labour laws, which provide workers with high levels of protection as well as strong formal bargaining rights, the South African economy has been increasingly affected by labour unrest. In 2010-2013, the country lost two to three times more man-days to strike action a year, compared with the late 1980s, when worker organisation formed an important part of the anti-apartheid struggle. In the third quarter of 2013, GDP growth plummeted to 0.6% from 3.2% in the first quarter and 0.8% in the second, largely as a result of widespread strikes in the mining and industrial sectors as well as declining business and investor confidence. This prompted economists to revise their annual growth forecasts for 2013 and 2014 down to 2% and even 1.8% – from 3% in 2010 and 2.5% in 2011.

The social environment

The economic environment has a major impact on the social environment, which determines the health, life expectancy, levels of education, and living standards of South Africans. Following the 1994 transition, the life expectancy of South Africans fell rapidly from 66 years in 1995 to 51 years in 2010, and subsequently stabilised at this level.[18] This compares very badly with the other BRICS countries, which recorded life expectancies of 73 (Brazil), 69 (Russia), 64 (India), and 73 (China).[19]

The reason for this can be traced back to the HIV and AIDS policies of the ANC government under Thabo Mbeki, which was responsible for thousands of unnecessary deaths, and which the former ANC MP Andrew Feinstein once described as 'irrational and criminal'.[20] The HIV-positive proportion of the adult population increased from 0.8% in 1991 to 10.9% in 2010.[21]

Of equal concern is the fact that very few people are well educated. In 2012 only 39% of adults had completed their school education, and only 6.5% had any tertiary education.[22] Various studies show that education standards in South African schools lag far behind those in its BRICS partners. Indeed, the World Economic Forum has ranked the quality of schooling in South Africa at 146th out of 148 countries – more or less on a par with Yemen.[23]

Despite the weak overall performance of the schooling

system, there are areas of progress. A relatively small number of blacks now attend former white schools, and research shows that they achieve results on a par with those of their white classmates.[24] As a result, the number of blacks in higher education more than doubled from 286 000 in 1995 to over 640 000 in 2013. This in turn has led to great increases in the number of black graduates. For example, while 303 blacks gained degrees in business and commerce in 1991, that figure increased to over 10 000 in 2013.[25] However, despite this progress, in 2012 only 4.1% of blacks older than 20 had any tertiary qualifications – as opposed to 25% of whites.[26]

This and other similar trends have led to the rise of a small black middle class. In 2012, according to a report published by the South African Presidency, 39% of senior managers were black.[27] A year earlier it was estimated that 35% of the value of all bonds, houses, listed shares, money market holdings, and non-residential property was in black hands, 41% was in white hands, and the balance was owned by foreigners and the state.[28] Likewise, roughly a third of suburban properties sold in South Africa in 2012 were bought by blacks.[29] IRR research due to be published in 2014 suggests that, while about 60%-70% of whites fall into the middle class, the figure for black South Africans is less than 10%.

Indicators such as poor health, high levels of unemployment and poor educational standards seem to suggest that living standards in South Africa have fallen since 1994. However, as pointed out previously, this is not the case. Since 1994, both the number and proportion of people and households with access to housing, water, and electricity increased hugely. Since 1994 the number of households living in formal houses increased by 5.4 million, and the proportion of households living in such houses from 64% to 78%.[30] Increases of a similar magnitude were recorded in respect of the supply of electricity and clean water. Moreover, in 2012, 15.5 million people, a third of the total population, were benefiting from social grants.[31] Despite these improvements in housing and access to grants life remains pretty desperate for South Africa's poor.

Trends in the social environment therefore suggest the presence of two prominent groups of people – which mirror the divides in the economic environment. The first is a relatively small group of citizens with good qualifications and a middle-class lifestyle. This is largely the same group – comprising about 10% of the population – identified in the economic environment as people with good jobs, and earning and spending relatively large amounts of money.

The second is the much larger group of people who, notwithstanding major improvements in their basic living standards, remain poor, badly educated, and largely dependent on welfare and service delivery funded by a minority of taxpayers.

A final point in respect of the social environment relates to demands for personal safety. In 2008 (the most recent year with comparable data), the other BRICS countries recorded murder rates per 100 000 people of 22 (Brazil), 14.2 (Russia), 2.8 (India), and 5.8 (China). In that year, the figure for South Africa was 36.5 – and it has since declined to 31. The social environment is therefore characterised by very high levels of violent crime,[32] and members of all social groupings are demanding higher levels of personal safety.

The political environment

The economic and social environments exist in conjunction with the political environment, which is populated by the government and by various political parties. The dominant political party is the ANC. In the first inclusive elections in 1994, the ANC, in alliance with COSATU and the SACP, won 62.7% of the national vote. It went on to increase its support to 65.9% in the fourth democratic national elections in 2009.

While national support for the DA – the official opposition – increased from just 2% in 1994 to more than 15% in 2009, it was still only a quarter of that of the ANC. The DA is currently the most prominent and influential of all the opposition parties. It wants to remove the ANC from power and remodel South African society. Other political parties have not managed to attract levels of support remotely approaching those for the DA and ANC.[33]

However, despite the dominance of the ANC – which claims to represent the interests of the majority of South Africans – growing numbers of citizens are turning to protest action. In 2012, there were 113 incidents of what were described as 'major' protests directed at the state – the study that identified these protests managed to find just ten incidents a decade earlier.[34] Many were marked by violence, with community members attacking government offices and other government property as well as public representatives of the ruling party. In 2010, by their own count, the police reported dealing with more than four incidents of voilent protest action a day.[35] With such levels of dissatisfaction things are bound to go wrong, as has happened on a number of occasions.

On 13 April 2011, Andries Tatane, a community activist in the town of Ficksburg in the Free State, was shot at close range by police during a service delivery protest, and died on the scene soon afterwards. Following this incident – which was widely televised, and provoked a national and international outcry – the IRR wrote to the Minister of Police, expressing its concern about growing community protests and increased police brutality in handling those protests, and stating its view that, if steps were not taken to modify police conduct, a massacre could occur.

In August 2013, just more than two years later, such a scenario materialised when a police task force armed with assault rifles, fatally shot more than 30 striking miners at Marikana in North West province, and wounded many others. The incident shocked the world (and the South African government), and provoked comparisons with the Sharpeville massacre of March 1960 when police opened fire on anti-apartheid protestors, killing 69 people. It caused huge damage to South Africa's international status and its reputation as a sound investment destination. Should the ANC lose a future election – as one of my scenarios will propose – this could be traced back in large part to the watershed in South African politics represented by the shooting at Marikana.

Had police management conducted a scenario exercise around growing community protests, one of them would certainly have thrown up an incident such as the shooting at Marikana. This would have allowed the SAPS to develop an appropriate strategy for dealing with these sorts of protests.

Therefore, besides the tripartite alliance and the official

opposition, a third important political actor is the growing protest movement. The number of actual and potential participants in this movement is obviously very difficult to estimate, but it is worth noting that the number of abstentions in the 2009 national election exceeded the number of votes for the ANC.

Other influential actors in the political environment are civil society and the media. In South Africa, both sectors are not only large, but also loud and vigorous, in their opposition to more and more of what the government is doing (or failing to do). For example, a 2006 study found that 51.1% of South Africans were members of a church or other religious organisation.[36] It also found that 7.2% belonged to a political party, 3.9% to an environmental organisation, 4% to a professional organisation, 5% to a charitable organisation, and 4.7% to a labour union. In 2010, there were 3 057 000 members of 200 registered trade unions. Besides this, in 2011 South Africa had 22 daily newspapers, 27 major weekly newspapers, 630 consumer magazines and newspapers, and 470 community newspapers.[37] The great majority of these were privately owned and edited.

The media and civil society exert considerable influence over the political system. For example, in September 2009 the civil rights group AfriForum secured a court order that forced the Pretoria City Council to restore electricity to schools whose supply had been severed because they had not paid their bills.[38] In December 2010, the *Mail & Guardian* won a court order forcing the government to give the newspaper a copy of a report on Zimbabwe's 2002 elections, which it had previously refused to do.[39] In July 2011, the Centre for

Social Accountability used the courts to gain access to official records relating to corruption by members of parliament who had abused their travel vouchers.[40] And in 2013 the Bisho High Court ordered the Minister of Basic Education to adopt minimum norms and standards for infrastructure in schools. This application was brought by the civil society group Equal Education in an attempt to improve poor infrastructure in South African schools.

These are all examples of how civil society and media groups are forcing the state to meet its constitutional obligations. These are not isolated incidents but rather part of a growing trend of citizens who are unhappy with the current state of South Africa and want to change it. In November 2011, a newspaper editorial noted that non-profit groupings were 'queuing up' to take the ANC to court wherever it overstepped its constitutional bounds.[41] That same year a Constitutional Court judge, Zak Yacoob, told a meeting at Wits University that civil society was obliged to 'examine proposed government and parliamentary conduct of every kind'.[42]

The analysis above suggests that a vast number of South Africans, including business leaders, politicians, and activists, favour some kind of change. In certain instances this might be a fairly modest degree of change, but the change wanted by the millions of poor is likely to be of a more dramatic nature. Knowing this, we now need to determine if such change can be brought about – both in terms of whether 'the rules of the game' in South Africa allow for it and whether role players have access to the required democratic institutions to effect such change.

The constitution and the bounty of citizens' rights

In South Africa the 'rules of the game' are firmly rooted in the constitution, and particularly the Bill of Rights embedded in it. For instance, while the ANC has almost unfettered political power to adopt new policies, it remains constrained by what the constitution allows. This applies to all individuals and groups, and determines which feedback mechanisms, such as elections, courts, or protest actions, they are able to use in seeking to transform the country.

Any assessment of the rules must first determine the extent to which they place limits on the actions of citizens and other actors when they make demands for change. Secondly, and equally importantly, we need to identify the boundaries within which the government is able to respond to those demands. We should also bear in mind that, in certain extreme scenarios, the rules themselves may be changed or discarded.

In South Africa today, perhaps the most significant of these rules is the right to equality, which requires that all citizens have equal opportunities for placing demands on the system, and that all their demands are treated equally. More specifically, the constitution holds that everyone is equal before the law and has a right to equal legal protection.[43] It describes equality as the 'full and equal enjoyment of all rights', and stipulates that legislative or other measures may be taken to protect a person disadvantaged by unfair discrimination on grounds ranging from race and gender to religion and culture. The emphasis here is on unfair discrimination and not on discrimination itself. This is because the constitution also holds that discriminatory measures, such as affirmative action, that seek redress for past wrongs, are not necessarily unfair. My colleague Anthea Jeffery has studied South Africa's performance in terms of its commitment to constitutional principles. According to her research, the right to equality is generally upheld, with examples including the Constitutional Court upholding the rights of same-sex couples, striking down the forced implementation of pre-paid water meters in Soweto, and striking down areas of customary law such as the male right to control property in a marriage.[44]

Besides equal treatment, citizens have the right to organise themselves into groups when making demands for change in how South Africa is run. This right is also important as it creates the boundaries within which individuals and groups can pursue change, and the ideas they may use in pursuit of such change. Broadly, these include the rights to freedom of religion, thought, opinion, expression, assembly, and demonstration; voting for public representatives, ultimately selecting a government; and the rights to form and campaign for political parties.[45] According to Jeffery, the political rights of individuals have generally been upheld, and the rights to freedom of speech and assembly have been strongly upheld.[46] Likewise, political commentators have argued that political rights are generally upheld, although certain role players are unaware of their rights.[47]

All citizens also have the right to own property, which is particularly significant in a society as unequal as South Africa's, and on a continent where private property rights often do not exist. This right protects the assets of the minority of relatively wealthy people, while promoting greater access to asset formation for the majority of relatively poor.

The property clause in the constitution prohibits the confiscation of property by the state, and requires compensation for any property that is expropriated, either for public purposes or in the public interest. However, the constitution also describes equitable access to land and property as being in the public interest, and stipulates that the state should introduce measures to enable citizens to gain such access. It also stipulates that the right to property cannot be used to impede the state's efforts to seek redress for past racial discrimination.[48]

Controversially, the constitution also provides a series of socio-economic rights, ranging from the right to housing to rights to food, education, and social security.[49] This provides the majority of relatively poor with specific mechanisms for making demands for socio-economic change that will improve their standards of living. However, the fact that you have a right to a house does not mean that a house exists for you to live in. In this respect the constitution requires the state to adopt 'reasonable legislative and other measures within its available resources to achieve the progressive realisation of these rights'. This is particularly significant in a society where more than a third of the population lives in relative poverty.

Finally, the constitution stipulates that any person has the right to have a dispute resolved by a fair public hearing in a court of law.[50] This is vital, as it means that demands need to be made and responded to in a legal framework, and not by edict or decree. According to Jeffery, these rights have also generally been upheld.[51]

In short: All South Africans have nearly equal rights to pursue their hopes, dreams, and aspirations and to be treated equally in the process. They have the right to organise themselves into groups in pursuit of change, and may express a wide range of ideas and opinions in the course of doing so. Property is protected against random seizure, while the government is obliged to seek ways of equalising access to resources. Moreover, all citizens have explicit socio-economic rights, which the government is obliged to pursue. Finally, all South Africans may expect that their demands for change will be responded to in terms of what the law allows and not by arbitrary executive decisions – politicians who make up regulations and policies as they go along.

You must be blind to South Africa's realities if you cannot see the contradiction that emerges here between this generous bounty of rights and freedoms and the poverty and deprived circumstances of so many people in the country. This contradiction suggests a country primed for radical change should its people have access to the mechanisms required to effect such change.

A plethora of feedback mechanisms

Considering South Africans' bounty of rights, it is hardly surprising that citizens have a wide array of mechanisms at their disposal to bring about change. To go back briefly to complex systems theory, these are the mechanisms people use to direct feedback into the society – and therefore to change it or to maintain the status quo. For this reason we often refer to these mechanisms as feedback mechanisms and they range from formal mechanisms, such as elections, to less formal but equally influential mechanisms like public protests.

The first and most obvious feedback mechanism is the electoral system. Several rounds of national, provincial, and local elections have been held since 1994. These have been contested by a broad range of political parties, and have widely been regarded as free and fair. They have attracted high (if declining – see elsewhere) levels of public participation, with some 13.6 million voting in the 2011 local government elections, comprising a turnout of 57%.[52] Elections are probably the single most important feedback mechanism in South Africa, as they allow individual actors to choose the government that they believe will best meet their demands.

A second significant mechanism is the courts. Since 1994, the Constitutional Court has considered no fewer than 565 cases.[53] Of these 217, or 38%, related to civil rights matters. In 152 or 40% of the 379 cases that have been concluded, the court found that the activities in question were indeed unconstitutional, and found in favour of the plaintiffs.

A prominent example is the Grootboom case heard by the Constitutional Court in 2009. Irene Grootboom was evicted from a shack in the informal settlement of Wallacedene on the outskirts of Cape Town without being offered alternative accommodation. She took her case to the Cape High Court, which ordered the state to provide her with housing. The state appealed against the order, and the matter went to the Constitutional Court. The court ruled that the state's housing policy was defective, in that it failed to provide housing to those in desperate need, and ordered the state to meet this obligation.[54]

A third important group of feedback mechanisms is the so-called Chapter 9 institutions. These are institutions established under chapter 9 of the constitution in order to entrench democracy. There are a number of these, but three play a particularly important role in allowing individuals and groups to change South Africa. Perhaps the most prominent (and popular) is the Office of the Public Protector, which has the power to investigate any action of any organ of state deemed to be improper.[55] It may report on the impropriety, and take remedial action.[56] Its current head, Advocate Thuli Madonsela, has received widespread support from both the media and civil society for her efforts in rooting out corruption and maladministration. Despite harsh government censure and criticism, she has stuck to her guns, claiming, in 2013, that President Jacob Zuma had misled parliament about state expenditure on his homestead at Nkandla in KwaZulu-Natal, and calling on him to repay inappropriate expenditure.

A second significant Chapter 9 institution is the South African Human Rights Commission (SAHRC). Its powers include monitoring and investigating human rights abuses, and taking remedial action where necessary. In July 2010, for example, the commission lodged papers with the Bloemfontein Equality Court on behalf of cleaning staff at the University of the Free State whose rights to dignity had been violated by students who had forced them to join a mock initiation ceremony.[57] And, also in 2010, the commission found the City of Cape Town guilty of rights abuses after it had neglected to enclose public toilets it had built for residents of local squatter camps.[58]

A third is the Office of the Auditor-General, which audits the financial statements of all national, provincial, and local authorities and organs of state. It has made findings of financial irregularity by public entities in all three spheres of government, and made them public. In 2013, it found that government departments had been responsible for wasteful and unauthorised expenditure to the tune of R30 billion.

Political parties themselves provide people with additional avenues for directing feedback. By utilising the internal structures of political parties, people are able to exercise considerable influence over the policies adopted by those parties. A case in point is the policy conferences of the ANC, which exert great influence over party and eventually government policy. The most prominent example was the axing of Thabo Mbeki as head of the ANC at that party's 2007 Polokwane electoral conference, which resulted in his resignation as South African president.

Political parties also play active roles in pursuing change – even outside of legislatures. In April 2011, the DA scored a political victory when the Supreme Court of Appeal declared that a meeting of the Judicial Service Commission, which decided not to continue disciplinary action against the Western Cape Judge President, John Hlophe, was not properly constituted.[59] In December 2011, again in response to a DA application, the Supreme Court of Appeal ruled that the Director of Public Prosecutions was not fit and proper to hold that post.[60]

The media and civil society also act as feedback mechanisms that enable people to demand changes to how South

Africa is run. As has been noted previously, more than half of South Africans belong to a civil society organisation, including churches. Data has also been cited on the vast numbers and reach of newspaper, radio, and television media in South Africa. Numerous cases have been cited of how people have used such mechanisms to place demands on the system.

In sum, there are six particularly prominent feedback mechanisms through which South Africans can try to change their country and the policies of its government, namely:

- Elections, which regularly allow citizens the opportunity to change their government.
- The courts, which have been used extensively by political parties, civil society, the media, and individual actors in pursuit of political, economic, and social change.
- The Chapter 9 institutions, especially the Public Protector, the Human Rights Commission, and the Auditor-General.
- The political parties themselves, which, especially in the case of the ANC, allow individuals to exert considerable influence over the policies adopted in the country.
- Public protests, an increasingly prominent strategy adopted by poor communities to register their demands for change.
- The media and civil society.

South Africa therefore finds itself at a critical juncture in the post-apartheid era. Citizens have access to a wide range of feedback mechanisms – yet the government remains in power despite its failure to meet popular expectations of a better life.

This takes us back to the two basic questions mentioned at the start of this chapter, namely whether South Africa's government is meeting the expectations of its citizens, and, if not, whether those citizens have the means to change the way in which the country is managed. The answer to the first question is a definite no. Even the many improvements in living standards achieved via state welfare and service delivery are hiking spiralling expectations that the government cannot hope to meet.

The answer to the second question is a definite yes. The current 'rules of the game' make it dead easy to bring change about – and the mechanisms to force such change are available to almost all South Africans.

Can there then still be any doubt that South Africa is headed for a second revolution – whichever form this may take?

THE POLICY PUZZLE

That fact that we could be headed for a second revolution suggests that something may be terribly wrong with the policies of government. What are its major policies, and how effective are they? If these policies are failing, why is this so? This is the fourth step in our scenario building exercise – to figure out how the government thinks, what it is trying to achieve, and whether its policies are capable of meeting the needs of its citizens.

In South Africa's case, public policy is made or influenced by two major role players. The first, obviously, is the government, which formulates policies in all the areas of public administration, publishes these in the form of green and white papers, translates them into legislation, and then seeks to implement them. The second is the ANC itself, which exerts active control over government policy via its own policy conferences, which are held every five years. Therefore, as is often the case in democratic systems, tensions sometimes arise between the ANC's policy recommendations and eventual government policies.

The government's current policies do not exist in a vacuum – they are the latest evolution in a series of policy frameworks developed and adopted since 1994. While at times these policies have been in conflict with one another, they ultimately reflect a small number of core ideas that have been present in all ANC and government policy-making since the mid-1990s. Tracing these ideas, and the threads that join them, will inform our understanding of the current policy framework, and how it may change in the future.

The Reconstruction and Development Programme (RDP)

The first major policy framework of the democratic era was the Reconstruction and Development Programme – a comprehensive socio-economic policy framework drawn up by the ANC-led tripartite alliance in consultation with many other organisations. Meant to serve as a developmental blueprint for building a post-apartheid South Africa, it was released a few weeks before the inaugural democratic elections in April 1994. In November 1994, the new ANC-led government (formally a government of national unity, which lasted until 1999) tabled a White Paper on Reconstruction and Development, based on the RDP 'base document'. It emphasised 12 policy goals, namely:

1. Achieving high and sustainable economic growth;
2. Privatising underutilised state assets;

3. Liberalising trade policy to boost exports;

4. Increasing employment via economic growth;

5. Reducing the budget deficit;

6. Financing the RDP via savings in other areas of government expenditure;

7. Increasing capital expenditure by government;

8. Forming a more effective civil service;

9. Reconstructing the environment of mainly black South Africans via the provision of housing, water, and electricity;

10. De-racialising the economy via legislation and policy changes in areas such as affirmative action;

11. Introducing competition policy to inhibit the overconcentration of economic power; and

12. Strengthening the bargaining position of labour.[1]

These 12 points contained three contrasting and even conflicting ideological strands. The first, reflected in points 1 to 6, comprised classic conservative macro-economic management aimed at stabilising the economy and stimulating economic growth. Thus in August 1995 the minister responsible for the RDP, Jay Naidoo, wrote that the RDP would be sourced from the national budget and not from borrowed money, and that growing the economy was one of the major programmes underpinning the RDP.[2] Similarly, in October 1996, the Minister of Finance, Trevor Manuel, wrote that a 'sound macroeconomic framework makes a comprehensive human development strategy possible'.[3]

The second strand, reflected in point 9, comprised the

state playing an active role in improving living standards by providing poor people with free or subsidised housing, electricity, and water. In the same article cited above, Naidoo wrote that the government wanted to build a million houses within five years. And Manuel wrote that the government was 'progressively effecting a redistribution of resources in education and health in favour of underserviced neighbourhoods'.[4]

The third strand, reflected in points 8, 10, 11, and 12, envisaged active government intervention in the economy in order to change the complexion of the ownership and management of economic resources, and to strengthen the bargaining position of labour. In October 1994 the Deputy Minister of Home Affairs, Penuell Maduna, declared that, unless business embraced the principles of reconstruction and development, the government would be forced to introduce affirmative action.[5] The RDP White Paper held that the government would take steps to 'discourage' financial institutions from discriminating in terms of race when it came to the lending of money. Furthermore, the government intended to 'regulate labour standards for small and medium enterprises'.[6]

The White Paper set up an elaborate system for implementing the RDP, co-ordinated by an RDP office headed by Naidoo, and involving a discrete RDP Fund. Despite intense attention to the RDP – which helped to fuel public expectations of rapid change under post-apartheid rule – the programme became bogged down in bureaucratic and other problems. In March 1996, faced with mounting frustrations and public criticism, President Nelson Mandela announced that the RDP office would be closed down, and that RDP programmes would be integrated into the main budgets and activities of all government departments and agencies. While the RDP has never been formally wound up or rescinded, it has effectively disappeared from the national policy discourse.

The Growth, Employment and Redistribution (GEAR) framework

In the same year, the government produced a second major policy framework, namely the macro-economic Growth, Employment and Redistribution framework. GEAR emphasised the importance of conservative macro-economic policies, possibly reflecting growing concerns within government that the economy would not reach the levels of growth necessary to fund its developmental and interventionist ambitions. Its key policy goals were to:

- Encourage greater public investment in infrastructure;
- Reduce the budget deficit;
- Use interest rates to control inflation;
- Relax exchange controls;
- Liberalise trade more rapidly;
- Introduce tax incentives to stimulate investment;
- Restrain growth of the public sector wage bill; and
- Privatise state-owned assets, and increase labour flexibility.[7]

GEAR therefore emphasised the conservative fiscal aspect of the RDP, especially with regard to trade liberalisation, public sector wage restraint, and labour market regulation. The

Sunday Independent described it as a 'broadly free-market economic policy'.[8] GEAR corresponded with resolutions adopted at the 1997 ANC policy conference at Mafikeng, which emphasised the importance of a 'fast-growing and developing economy' and the 'promotion of investment for sustainable jobs'. While conference resolutions also cited the importance of a redistribution of wealth, they emphasised the 'continuous link between growth and development'.[9] However, this was the last ANC policy conference that condoned such a conservative macro-economic approach.

To the extent that GEAR was aimed at accelerating economic growth, it initially failed to achieve the desired result. From 1994 to 1999, levels of GDP growth were far too low to make inroads into poverty and unemployment,[10] and it became increasingly clear that the government was failing to meet the demands of the relatively poor 50% of South Africans. Indeed, the proportion of South Africans living on less than $2 per day had increased from 12.1% in 1994 to 15.5% in 1999,[11] unemployment had increased from 20% to 23%, and the number of unemployed black (African) South Africans had increased from 1 637 000 to 2 751 000.[12]

On 7 June 2001, *Business Day* stated in an editorial that GEAR had 'failed to realise rapid economic growth or any other of the promises in its title'. GEAR also provoked increasing opposition from other quarters, some of them within the tripartite alliance. As early as 1996 the then general secretary of COSATU, Sam Shilowa, accused the government of forcing South Africa in 'a direction diametrically opposed to the growth path of the RDP'.[13] In December 1997, this and other similar attacks forced Manuel to argue that GEAR did not contradict the RDP, but rather served as a means of realising its developmental goals.[14]

On 29 June 1998, the *Cape Argus* noted in an editorial that the SACP and COSATU had denounced GEAR and had won some support from church leaders in doing so. In response, Mandela launched a sharply worded attack on the ANC's alliance partners.[15] Many analysts, including those at the IRR, agreed that this defence was justified as GEAR represented an effective macro-economic framework that would stabilise the economy, bolster investor confidence, and stimulate private sector-led economic growth. However, criticism from the ANC's alliance partners continued, prompting *Business Day* to observe, some three years later, that '[Trevor] Manuel is increasingly feeling the heat from the left, as critics, including the ANC's trade union allies, slate government for its religious commitment to fiscal discipline'.[16]

Manuel was effectively left to bat for GEAR on his own, with very little popular or political support. Only a handful of think-tanks, including the IRR, came to his defence. Many civil society organisations criticised or rejected GEAR, fuelling negative popular sentiment, as reflected in the media. Business leaders that could have backed GEAR in order to save Manuel kept their heads below the parapet for fear of 'getting involved in politics' – ignoring the fact that, if you continue to avoid getting involved in politics, politics might find a way of involving itself with you.

There can be little doubt that the low levels of business confidence and high levels of uncertainty with which the South

African business community has to cope today have their origins in this attitude. Had the business community stood up at that time – not against the government, but in support of its friends in the government – it would have profited from a far more positive investment environment. We regularly make this point in dealing with business leaders who ask us to advise them on how to go about shaping a more favourable investment policy environment. They do not like to hear it, and most still reject it.

Tensions over GEAR came to a head at the ANC's policy conference held in Stellenbosch in December 2002. After heated debates, delegates adopted a series of resolutions on economic policy, many of which contradicted GEAR. They emphasised five policy goals, namely to:

- Tackle poverty and unemployment via a more comprehensive social welfare programme;
- Reduce unemployment via a public works programme;
- Review land ownership patterns with a view to discouraging foreign ownership of land;
- Promote BEE as an 'economic requirement' of South Africa's future; and
- Intervene directly in various industries in order to promote equity and black management and ownership within those industries.[17]

In other words, the conference emphasised the interventionist and developmental strands of ANC and government policy. As a result, government policy became increasingly interventionist, especially in respect of racial transformation. My colleague Anthea Jeffery cites four major instances:[18]

The first comprised changes to labour legislation that made it more difficult to employ casual workers; introduced minimum wages for domestic, agricultural, and trade and retail workers; and placed various restrictions on retrenchments. Jeffery notes that the last-named provision was intended to prevent private sector takeovers of inefficient public sector corporations.

The second was the introduction of the Mineral and Petroleum Resources Development Act (2002), aimed at providing for 'equitable access to and the sustainable development of the nation's mineral and petroleum resources',[19] which effectively nationalised South Africa's mineral assets. The Act required the development of a 'broad-based socio-economic empowerment charter', or mining charter, aimed at 'effecting the entry of historically disadvantaged South Africans into the mining industry', and allowing them to benefit from the exploitation of mining and mineral resources. The first mining charter, also released in 2002, required mining companies to reapply for their mining rights, which were not guaranteed but could be granted for 30 years if the companies in question complied with various black economic empowerment stipulations. South Africa's most respected expert in mining law, Peter Leon (brother of the former DA leader, Tony Leon), described the legislation as an 'ill-conceived brew of ministerial excess ... at odds with the government's promotion of a market economy'.[20]

The third was the introduction of the Promotion of Equality

and Prevention of Unfair Discrimination Act (2002), which sought to prevent unfair income differentials and red-lining by commercial banks – the very thing the White Paper on the RDP had said it would discourage the banks from doing.

The fourth was the introduction of the Broad Based Black Economic Empowerment Act (2003), which requires businesses to meet various racial targets in respect of ownership, management, procurement, and employment.

However, the interventionist approach did not deliver results. Rates of economic growth remained pedestrian,[21] and unemployment increased even further, from 23% in 1999 to 28% in 2004. The number of unemployed black (African) South Africans increased from 2 751 000 to 3 681 000 in the same period.[22] However, the accelerated roll-out of welfare programmes marginally reduced the poverty rate measured at $2 per day from 15.5% in 1999 to 13%.[23]

The Accelerated and Shared Growth Initiative for South Africa (AsgiSA)

In 2006, largely in response to this poor economic performance, the government announced the Accelerated and Shared Growth Initiative for South Africa. Its main goals were to:

- Introduce greater labour market flexibility via a review of labour laws;
- Promote/encourage investment in infrastructure;
- Ensure a more competitive business environment especially for small and medium-sized enterprises;

- Achieve GDP growth of 4.5% by 2009 and 6% between 2010 and 2014;
- Improve the value of the rand;
- Review BEE policy; and
- Ensure a supply of skilled labour.[24]

Launching the initiative, the deputy president, Phumzile Mlambo-Ngcuka, said the government had calculated that a growth rate of at least 5% was needed to allow it to meet its social objectives, and that the 'environment and opportunities for more labour-absorbing economic activities [needed to be] considerably improved'.[25]

The emphasis had therefore swung back from the interventionist and developmental end of the spectrum to the conservative one, even going as far as proposing a review of interventionist and regulatory mechanisms such as BEE and labour market regulations that had followed the Stellenbosch conference. However, as could be expected, AsgiSA provoked strong resistance from both COSATU and the SACP. When, in September 2006, the Minister of Provincial and Local Government, Sydney Mufamadi, tried to explain the government's economic policy to a COSATU congress, he was heckled to the point where he was forced to leave the stage.[26] Again, business leaders largely remained silent.

The thrust of COSATU's criticism was that adherence to fiscal discipline was benefiting the rich at the expense of the poor. Besides Manuel, President Thabo Mbeki defended both GEAR and AsgiSA. In December 2007, however, at the ANC's momentous policy conference at Polokwane, Mbeki was voted out as president of the ANC, prompting his resignation as South African president in September the next year. The conference also adopted a series of resolutions that once again swung the pendulum away from the conservative end of the spectrum towards the interventionist end. These resolutions emphasised the following seven policy priorities:

- A greater role for the state in directing investment and economic policy;
- A centralised state planning agency;
- intervention in the private ownership of land to ensure more equitable access to property;
- The deployment of members of the ANC to all sectors of the economy in order for the party 'as the strategic centre of power' to exercise 'leadership over society in pursuit of the National Democratic Revolution';
- Regulating the foreign ownership of land;
- Strengthening the role of parastatals (businesses owned and run by the state) in directing economic activity; and
- Further expanding social welfare.[27]

This meant that the pendulum had swung back further in the direction of direct state interventionism than at any other point since 1994. The ANC drafted its 2009 election manifesto against this background. In line with the Polokwane conference resolutions, the ANC committed itself to eight policy goals.

The first was a strongly interventionist state that would direct economic activity. The second was to create employment via 'a massive programme of expanded public works', and to increase unemployment insurance. The third was to promote more free services from government. The fourth was to accelerate land reform. The fifth was to promote the role of the state in investing in industry. The sixth was to 'vigorously' implement further black empowerment and affirmative action policies. The seventh was to further tighten labour market regulation. The eighth was to introduce free National Health Insurance.[28]

Thus it appeared as if developmental and interventionist policy goals had largely taken the place of conservative macro-economic ones. This was despite the fact that the post-AsgiSA economy had begun to show signs of achieving the levels of growth the government had been pursuing since 1994.[29] As a result, the absolute number of unemployed people had declined from a high of 4 843 000 in 2003 to 4 119 000 in 2007 – the first and only absolute and sustained decline in unemployment since 1994.[30] Moreover, the budget deficit had been reduced from a high of 5.1% in 1996 to surpluses of 0.7% and 0.9% in 2007 and 2008 respectively[31] – an extraordinary achievement for a developing economy.

The surpluses were recorded despite the fact that the government's developmental policies were reaching more and more people. For example, by 2007 the government had built 2.3 million houses for poor households.[32] Moreover, the number of children benefiting from social grants had increased from fewer than 1 million to just under 8 million over the decade to 2007.[33] The proportion of South Africans living on less than $2 per day had halved from 13% in 2004 to 6.7% in 2009.[34]

Therefore, while the post-AsgiSA economy had allowed

the ANC to meet the demands of ordinary South Africans and investors more effectively than at any other point since 1994, the Polokwane conference had seen the party abandon what was beginning to look like a winning policy formula. Admittedly, despite the progress made, a number of obstacles to future growth were beginning to manifest themselves.

Debt as a proportion of disposable income of households increased from 56.5% in 1994 to 81% in 2009.[35] As a result, savings as a proportion of the after-tax income of households had fallen into negative territory.[36] Following the global financial crisis, the economy contracted by 1.5% in 2009 – its first negative performance since 1992.[37] The unemployment rate, while lower than the 27.9% recorded in 2004, remained stubbornly high at 23.5% – higher than the rate in 1994.[38]

Perhaps recognising some of these successes, the Zuma administration did not completely abandon the macroeconomic conservatism of GEAR and AsgiSA. For example, Zuma retained Manuel as cabinet minister, giving him the influential planning portfolio. However, he also made room for proponents of a more centrally directed economy, such as Rob Davies as Minister of Trade and Industry, and Ebrahim Patel as Minister of Economic Development. Patel joined the government straight from the trade union movement, which had sharply criticised economic policy under Mbeki.

The New Growth Path (NGP)

Rather unsurprisingly, given the diverging ideological currents reflected in these appointments, the post-2009 government soon produced two different and largely contradictory policy frameworks. The first of these was the New Growth Path, masterminded by Patel and published in November 2011. Its main goals were to:

- Enable the state to play a leading role in directing investment and providing investment incentives;
- Promote domestic investment;
- Promote employment via the private sector;
- Promote public sector investment in infrastructure;
- Target labour-absorbing industries for investment;
- Promote small-scale agriculture;
- Review BEE policy to focus on skills development and worker and community ownership;
- Increase labour market regulation to protect vulnerable workers;
- Resist the reduction of trade tariffs while promoting exports and combating illegal imports; and
- Cap management salaries at R500 000 a year, and moderate the pay increases for people earning between R3 000 and R20 000 a month.

The rest of the NGP involved the same commitments to promoting skills, reducing unemployment, curbing poverty, and providing better services as had featured in all government policy frameworks since 1994.[39]

Clearly, the NGP envisaged an interventionist state, playing an active role in directing economic activity. While it spoke of private sector job creation, this goal was contradicted by the goal of increasing labour market regulation. In an editorial on 2 December 2011, *Business Day* observed that the document had shocked the business community, and suggested that some people in government still needed to learn that 'ideology does not work in the real world'.

The National Development Plan (NDP)

Within a month, the National Planning Commission, working under Manuel, produced another major policy framework, namely the National Development Plan.[40] Notably, it questioned the capacity of the state to lead investment and create jobs – the premise of the New Growth Path (NGP). Policy goals were to:

- Maintain fiscal discipline and macro-economic stability;
- Achieve sustained GDP growth of 5.4%;
- Reduce unemployment to 14% by 2020 and to 6% by 2030;
- Overhaul the civil service to improve efficiency and implementation;
- Promote market competitiveness;
- Reduce the cost of living;
- Reduce impediments to investment; and
- Create jobs via entrepreneurship and reduced regulation as well as a public works programme.

At first, the National Development Plan (NDP) was widely welcomed. Sanlam's chief economist, Jac Laubscher, wrote that it displayed 'a remarkable willingness to face up to the hard realities facing South Africa', challenging the New Growth Path's 'blind faith in the state'. He added that the NDP was 'clear in its vision that the private sector is the key role player in the economy.'[41]

However, while the NDP undoubtedly displays a willingness to face up to the realities facing South Africa, it does not show a willingness to face up to what must be done to overcome these realities – and hike economic growth above 5%. For example, while seeking to secure property rights, the plan also suggested that farmers should surrender 20% of their property at below market prices. It sought to boost job creation, but did not propose major labour market reforms. It sought to secure increased investment, but was unwilling to abandon punitive racial policy quotas and targets. In other words, it tinkered with existing policies, many of which had failed, while expecting significantly different social and economic outcomes. Therefore, it was neither a reformist document in the mould of GEAR, nor a road map to socialism in the mould of the New Growth Path.

John Kane-Berman, after spending many months studying the NDP (an experience he equated to trekking through a mangrove swamp), described it best by saying it was 'neither fish nor fowl' and that it had a 'ja-nee' (ja well, no fine) approach to turning our economy around. It is not, therefore, the dramatic policy turnaround that South Africa needs to meet the expectations of its people – a fact which to this day very few analysts are prepared to acknowledge.

Reformers versus statists

It may seem as if the ANC government and the ANC itself have pursued a bewildering array of policy goals and frameworks since 1994. However, when these frameworks are dissected, it emerges that the government's policy position is somewhat less complex than it appears to be at first sight. More specifically, it has pursued three policy threads simultaneously, emphasising different ones at different times. This pattern has continued into the era of President Jacob Zuma.

- The **developmental policy** thread seeks to meet the demands of those who are poorly educated, not active in the labour market, and dependent on welfare.
- The **growth policy** thread seeks to stimulate the economic growth, investment, and tax revenues needed to implement the policies of the government.
- The **interventionist policy** thread seeks to direct investment and business activity towards the government's developmental goals.

We can further simplify the policy puzzle facing the South African government by placing its supporters in just two camps. In the one camp we have what I call the reformers. This group realises that the redistributive and welfare model of development used in South Africa for the past 20 years has run out of road. While it has improved basic living standards, it has not created jobs or given people the education they need to take charge of their own lives and improve their own circumstances. It only drives up popular expectations, without securing the investment and economic growth to meet those expectations. The reformist camp is starting to understand that what South Africa needs is investment, growth, and entrepreneurship to create jobs – and not more redistribution. They favour a smaller role for the state.

In the other camp you will find the statists. They believe popular dissatisfaction can be attributed to the fact that the state has not gone far enough yet in redistributing wealth and that it should play a bigger role in the economy. They argue the state needs to intervene more directly in the economy, both as a player and as a referee to take wealth, jobs, businesses, and land from people who have such things and give them to people who do not.

These two camps, while part of the same government, are at opposite extremes when it comes to their ideas on how to run a country or grow an economy.

Interestingly, there is a precedent for such a policy split in South African history since the Afrikaners faced a similar division in the latter decades of apartheid. In the late 1960s, Dr Wimpie de Klerk, then editor of *Die Transvaler*, and brother to the later state president FW de Klerk, coined the terms 'verligtes' and 'verkramptes' to describe two broad strands in Afrikaner thinking about government policy and South Africa's future. Essentially, the *verligtes* (literally, the enlightened) were more liberal and progressive, and the *verkramptes* (the narrow-minded) were arch-conservative. Broadly, the *verligtes* recognised that apartheid had run into such difficulties that a completely different set of future policies had to be negotiated, while the *verkramptes* stubbornly refused to entertain any meaningful reforms.

We see similar divisions emerging within the ANC as the ruling party is confronted with its own policy puzzle. The 'new *verligtes*' or reformers favour market-friendly reforms, while the 'new *verkramptes*' or statists favour more redistribution, increased economic regulation, and greater state intervention in the economy. The new *verligtes* realise, once again, that the government is in an increasingly difficult position, and that growth and jobs are the only way out.

Just as the battle between the original *verligtes* and *verkramptes* in Afrikaner ranks shaped South Africa's future up to the political transition, the battle between the new *verligtes* and new *verkramptes* within the tripartite alliance will shape our policy future over the next decade.

KEY TRENDS IN SOUTH AFRICAN SOCIETY

★ ★ ★

Let us recap where we are in terms of the ten steps to building scenarios. Before anything else, we had to determine what we want to achieve. In this case, we want to know what it will be like to live in a future South Africa.

The second step was to find out if South Africans are satisfied with the status quo. We determined that the majority of people are in fact intent on bringing about significant change. The third step was to ask whether they have the means to bring such change about, and we established that they indeed have a wide range of change mechanisms available.

The fourth step was to understand the policy environment in the country, and why government policy is not meeting people's expectations. Here we found that the government was at odds with itself about how to meet these expectations, with some officials favouring a state-led economy while others favour a market-driven economy. The resultant policy puzzle has *paralysed government to quite an extent and has led to a slow-down in economic growth and investment.*

Our fifth step will be to take all the information we have gathered so far and in this chapter begin to identify key trends. These trends will later shape the highways we will follow into the future.

I am privileged to work with an outstanding team of researchers who do a sterling job in tracking and diagnosing political, economic and social trends for South Africa. This is a tradition at the IRR that extends back to the early 1930s when we published our first annual survey of the state of South Africa. It grew into the behemoth *South Africa Survey* that we still publish today, with about 900 pages of political, economic, and social data. The survey has a very proud record – among others, Nelson Mandela quoted from it in his famous 'I am prepared to die' speech from the dock in 1964 – and it remains a unique guide to the state of South Africa. In writing this chapter, I am in the fortunate position of being able to draw heavily on the survey – and other work by my colleagues.

We already know we are living in an unusual society that is both very unequal and very free. Exactly how this contradiction will play itself out is one of the key issues we need to resolve in the course of building our scenarios. Various outcomes are possible. The economy could grow far more rapidly, thus reducing inequality as well as its political risks. Alternatively, persistent inequality could trigger a second revolution in which the freedoms we have enjoyed since

1994 will be stripped away. Mapping out these plausible alternative futures requires identifying key current political, economic, and social trends that will serve as a factual basis for the scenarios themselves – the fifth step in our scenario building exercise.

As you are about to experience, this step can often be a bewildering and confusing exercise, due to the volume and contradictory nature of the information we need to bring into our analysis. But do not despair – the chapters that follow will bring order to the chaos, and, with that, a clear sense of what will happen in South Africa over the next ten years.

Political trends

As we saw in chapter 5, the ANC has dominated national, provincial, and local politics since 1994, mustering substantial absolute majorities in all the national elections. While its share of the vote weakened slightly from 69.7% in 2004 to 65.9% in 2009, it is still on par with its 66.3% in 1999, and higher than its 62.6% in 1994.[1] The ANC's dominance of the political arena is a key trend that will play an important role in determining South Africa's future.

The second most important party-political role player is the DA. Support for the DA and its forerunner, the Democratic Party (DP), has escalated from 1.7% of votes cast in 1994 to 9.6% in 1999, 12.4% in 2004, and 16.7% in 2009. Among other things, it has benefited from the demise of the NP, which garnered 20.4% of the vote in 1994, and its successor, the New National Party (NNP), which disbanded in 2005.[2] If the Congress of the People (COPE) had not been formed, gathering 7.4% of the vote in 2009, the DA would probably have won more than 20% of the national vote, and have been even more influential today.

The trend for other opposition parties is that they have shrunk dramatically since 1994. Support for the NNP slid from 6.9% in 1999 to 1.7% in 2004 before remnants of the party merged with the ANC, and support for the IFP more than halved from 10.5% in 1994 to 4.6% in 2009.[3] An obvious trend, then, is that South African politics has developed into an effective two-party system, even though the larger of these two parties attracts almost four times the support of the smaller one.

A less obvious, and poorly understood, trend is that the ANC has weakened significantly at the same time. This emerges when ANC support is measured not as a percentage of votes cast but as a percentage of potential votes – in other words, all people who are eligible to vote, whether or not they register or turn out at the polls. While in 1994 the ANC won 53.9% of the potential vote, this dropped to 47% in 1999, 40% in 2004, and 38% in 2009.[4]

This decline is linked to a sustained rise in the abstention rate – the number of people who are eligible to vote, but do not turn up at the polls. In 1994, 19.5 million of 22.7 million potential voters cast valid votes. In 2009, however, only 17.9 million of some 30 million potential voters cast valid votes. In other words, voter turnout had declined from 86% to 59%. Among other things, this means that, in 2009, the 41% of people who did not vote outstripped the 38% who voted for the ANC.[5]

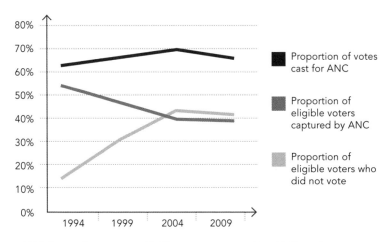

ANC share of votes cast, eligible voters captured by ANC, and proportion of eligible voters who did not vote, 1994–2009

Abstention rates are of great interest to political analysts as they serve as indicators of political participation – or, put the other way around, of political apathy, disillusionment, or passive political protest. South Africa's rapidly growing army of absent voters is certainly a very significant trend, but not a sign of political apathy. The decline in political participation has coincided with a sharp rise in so-called service delivery protests at the community level, as outlined in chapter 5. Taken together, this development reflects growing popular disillusionment with, and a loss of support for, the ANC and the government it leads.

While declining support is one clear threat to its future, growing divisions within the party are another. In fact, the political infighting in the ANC often seems more intense – and more significant – than the contestation between the ANC and other political parties. In 2012, a South African journalist, Gareth van Onselen, identified 20 separate ANC congresses, or other gatherings, since 2008, where delegates had come to blows.[6] More seriously, the former general secretary of COSATU, Zwelinzima Vavi, has claimed that numerous alliance leaders have been assassinated as a result of internal turmoil.[7]

Tensions surrounding Vavi himself are a good example of the extent of infighting within the tripartite alliance. Over the years, Vavi gained increasing prominence as a forceful and independent role player who did not hesitate to criticise goings-on in national politics or within the tripartite alliance. In August 2013 he was suspended as general secretary of COSATU after admitting to an affair with a young office clerk whom he had helped to hire. However, the record shows that the alliance partners do not often suspend their leaders, even when they have been implicated in criminal conduct. Rumour had it that Vavi's suspension had more to do with power politics in the tripartite alliance than with sexual morality. Put differently, it appeared as if the ANC, SACP, and elements of COSATU were acting in concert to force Vavi out of power, and replace him with a more malleable figure. This is exactly what the ANC did in 2012 when it suspended the leadership of the ANC Youth League on spurious charges and later dismissed them, making way for 'new' leaders who supported Jacob Zuma and his administration.

In the cloak-and-dagger world of the tripartite alliance, the daggers are often all too real. IRR research shows that, in the five years up to 2012, as many as 46 political leaders were assassinated.[8] The conflict, plotting, intrigue, and internal suspicion is also not a recent phenomenon. In his book *South Africa: The First Man, The Last Nation*, the noted analyst and historian RW Johnson recalls the 'absurd' allegation by former president Thabo Mbeki that senior ANC leaders Mathews Phosa, Cyril Ramaphosa, and Tokyo Sexwale were plotting against him 'with the connivance of foreign intelligence services'.[9] A number of ANC supporters, especially those who dislike Jacob Zuma, like to refer to the Mbeki era as a better time for the ANC. But all too often the current rot in the party can be traced back to that era and even earlier. Infighting and internal leadership turmoil is one prominent example of a long-term trend.

This trend points to another major political trend, namely that constant infighting may increasingly weaken and even paralyse the ruling party to the point that it can no longer make coherent policy and therefore save itself. The scale of the infighting, and the fact that it has extended to political assassination, means that this infighting is also an important driver of feedback into the political system. This is significant as it suggests that the party, and the broader alliance of which it forms a part, may find it difficult to unite behind a single set of policy proposals in an effort to meet the expectations of its remaining supporters.

The reason for this is that many key members of the ANC – and its alliance partners – remain at odds over how best to respond to rising levels of popular dissatisfaction. Some leading figures – notably in COSATU and the SACP – argue that the state should play a more active role in national development. Others, such as Trevor Manuel and Cyril Ramaphosa, appear to favour a private sector-led growth model, with the state playing a secondary role.

Part of the ANC's current policy dyslexia may relate to its rather murky underlying ideological framework. In terms of its current constitution, the party formally supports a National Democratic Revolution (NDR), defined as the 'process of transforming the country from an apartheid state to a non-racial, non-sexist, united democratic society in which all people enjoy equal rights'.[10]

Support for the NDR is also the founding principle of the tripartite alliance. This seems like a desirable objective that corresponds with the South African constitution.

But, as Blade Nzimande, general secretary of the SACP and Minister of Higher Education and Training, has publicly acknowledged, the concept of the NDR emanates from Marxism-Leninism and its aims are more sinister. The NDR can be understood as a 'revolution led by progressive forces ... (mainly oppressed and exploited) ... to defeat repressive and colonial regimes and build people's democracies, as both an objective in itself, but also in circumstances where ... such a revolution is unable to immediately proceed to socialism'.[11]

In this framework – spelled out in some detail in the SACP's programme entitled The Path to Power, which appears on its website – apartheid South Africa was and is regarded as an example of colonialism (albeit 'Colonialism of a Special Type, because, unlike others, the 'colonial ruling class with its white support base and the oppressed colonial majority are located within a single country').[12] This, in turn fits into Lenin's theory of imperialism, which holds that the wealth of colonial powers is derived from the exploitation of their colonies, and is therefore illegitimate.

As a result, left-leaning members of the ANC believe that property and other forms of wealth held by white 'colonists' are illegitimate and should therefore be restored to the black majority (or the state), even at the cost of economic growth. Some analysts have suggested that the ANC's continued commitment to the notion of the NDR may even contravene the South African constitution.[13] There is ample material that could be used to support this claim. For example, an ANC discussion paper released before the 2012 National Policy Conference speaks of the need for a 'second transition', building on the foundation of South Africa's political transformation, as the first transition had proven 'inadequate and even inappropriate for a social and economic transformation phase'.[14] It goes on to propagate a 'developmental state that plays a driving role in the social and economic development of the country'.[15] For its part, the SACP makes it clear that it regards the National Democratic Revolution as an interim stage on the way to establishing a socialist South Africa and, ultimately, a 'classless communist society'.[16]

Economic trends

Political trends are, of course, largely a product of the economic environment; this is why business people who say they want nothing to do with politics often end up facing major economic problems. It is this environment that determines South Africa's prosperity or otherwise, and therefore its ability to meet the demands placed upon it by citizens.

Economic growth is a key factor in any society as it determines the extent to which economic opportunities are created for role players in the system, as well as the extent of tax revenue available for redistribution by the state in the form of services and welfare. However, it is widely agreed that levels of economic growth are half of what they need to be in order to make significant inroads into poverty and unemployment.[17] They are also about half of those in the other BRICS countries. In fact, in 2013 South Africa was one of the five slowest growing economies in Africa. This may not change, as there are at least seven structural impediments to economic growth.

The first is the low savings rate, measured in relation to GDP, which impedes capital formation (or money that is available to invest) and therefore productive investment. While savings comprised 16.8% of GDP in 1994, it was fractionally lower at 16.4% in 2010 – far below the 52% of China and the 22% of Brazil.[18] As early as July 2011 the Minister of Finance, Pravin Gordhan, warned that South Africa's low savings rate was holding the economy back compared with its peers, and that a savings rate closer to 25% of GDP was needed to achieve higher levels of sustainable growth.[19]

The second constraint on growth is high levels of household debt, which have escalated rapidly in recent years.[20] In 1994, for example, household debt as a percentage of disposable income was 57%. This rose quickly to reach 82% by 2008, declining marginally to 76% in 2012. This means that domestic consumer expenditure is unable to act as a major driver of future economic growth because consumers' high debt levels now constrain their ability to spend money.

The third constraint is that South Africa is lagging behind other developing markets in attracting foreign direct investment (FDI).[21] For example, in 2012 foreign investors made up just 6% of fixed investment into the South African economy (investment in, for instance, new factories) compared with 15% in Brazil and 12% in Russia.

The fourth constraint is the ongoing budget deficit, or the extent to which the government's expenditure exceeds its revenue, or income from taxes and the like. In 2010 the budget deficit equalled 5.5% of GDP, a very high level even when compared with the turbulent 1970s and 1980s.[22] By 2013 this figure was still hovering around 5% of GDP, which was considerably higher than the 2.7% of Brazil, 2% of China, and 0.5% of Russia.[23] In 2013, a country in deep financial distress such as Spain averaged a deficit of 7.1%.[24] This shows that the South African government is struggling to fund the policies it has adopted in an effort to meet the expectations of its supporters, and has to borrow money to meet these commitments and promises. There is therefore limited room to increase government expenditure, such as that on infrastructure, aimed at stimulating economic growth.

A fifth constraint is the quality and availability of skills, which will be addressed in greater detail further on. A sixth constraint is poor infrastructure. For example, in 2011 the Minister of Transport, Ben Martins, told parliament that only 70 000 of the 153 000 kilometres of paved roads in South Africa were in a good or very good condition.[25] In 2009, more than 1.3 billion tonnes of freight was transported on South Africa's roads compared with 173 million tonnes carried on the railways.[26] This suggests that rail freight infrastructure is inadequate, forcing freight to be carried on the road network, which is much more expensive. In fact, between 2007 and 2009, freight carried by rail declined by 16%.[27]

But the most serious infrastructure constraint of all relates to electricity supply. In 2008, inadequate electricity generation capacity forced Eskom to introduce a programme of 'rolling blackouts', at great cost to the economy. In early 2012, several mining companies shut down some of their smelters in order to help Eskom manage its inadequate power supply[28] – despite the importance the government has attached to the beneficiation of minerals, and the criticism it has levelled at mining houses for not beneficiating more. While a number of new power stations are due to come on line, at 4% demand growth, electricity demand is again expected to exceed supply by 2019.[29]

The seventh constraint on growth is low levels of entrepreneurship. In 2009, only 1.4% of South Africans aged 15-64 owned established businesses, against 13.5% in Brazil, 2.3% in Russia, and 17.2% in China.[30] A 2012 study suggested that the new business ownership rate in South Africa, which measures what proportion of people are successfully establishing a new business that pays them an income, was a quarter of the figure for Brazil and half of that for China, and well below that of countries ranging from Slovakia to Latvia and Malaysia.[31]

A major risk factor emanating from low levels of economic growth, and poor domestic economic activity, is a large current account deficit. The current account reflects the difference in value between a country's imports and exports. A current account deficit arises when the value of imported goods and services exceeds the value of exported goods and services, and the country in question has to borrow the difference on international money markets.

This is no different from a household budget deficit, when a household spends more than its members are earning – forcing them to borrow money to make ends meet. As in the case of households, when a country can no longer service its debts from its income, it effectively becomes insolvent. When current account deficits start reaching danger levels, ratings agencies start warning international investors to steer clear of the country concerned, thus creating the risk that its currency may suffer a precipitous decline in value.

In South Africa's case this has not happened yet because of so-called portfolio flows. This is money flowing into the country from international investors seeking to take advantage of South Africa's interest rates, which are 5-6 percentage points higher than those in Europe and America. Therefore, they can gamble by borrowing money at low interest rates in Europe and investing it in South Africa. This is hot money that can be withdrawn at the click of a mouse – yet it plays a vital role in balancing South Africa's current account. If interest rates rise elsewhere in the world, or fall in South Africa, this flow of money may dry up, with the result that South Africa will risk being regarded as bankrupt. The only sure way to overcome this risk is to increase exports, but in South Africa's case this is constrained by poor skills, poor productivity, high input costs, and poor international competitiveness. All this amounts to what we call the 'interest rate trap'.

Moreover, government service delivery as well as public investment is constrained by a relatively small tax base. In 2010 there were only 5.9 million registered taxpayers, but this number rose to 13.7 million by 2012. However, this latter figure is dangerously misleading as it results not from a growth in the tax base, but rather from the fact that from 2011 it became compulsory for all employees to be registered for income tax. At the Centre for Risk Analysis we had previously estimated that of the 6 million or so actual income taxpayers 40% earned less than R120 000 a year, and 90% earned less than R400 000 a year. In fact, 60% of taxable income was earned by people earning less than R400 000 a year.[32]

Therefore, a relatively small number of people are providing the government with the tax revenue it needs to implement its policies. On top of that, the tax burden is disproportionate within this small group. We estimate that 2% of the adult population pays more than 50% of income tax received by the state. Among other things, this is used to pay more than 15 million social grants, which help to support in the region of 50% of all the households in South Africa. Therefore the government dares not maltreat the middle classes (too much) for fear of losing this valuable source of income, which helps it to retain the support of many poor people.

High unemployment rates preclude any prospect of a dramatic increase in the size of the tax base in the short to medium term. Since 2001 the employment rate – the proportion of the population of working age that is actually employed – has fallen from 45.8% to 40.6%.[33] In fact, from 2001 to 2011, the number of employed South Africans increased from 12.5 million to just 13.1 million, even though the population of working age increased by more than 5 million people.[34] Current unemployment levels – which are highest among young people, thus affecting their perceptions of their futures – are recorded in chapter 4.

As a result, job creation is a priority in the minds of most South Africans. For example, a March 2011 poll found that 90% of all South Africans, and 95% of black males, believed job creation was South Africa's most pressing need.[35] This places economic growth at the centre of the social equation – we need the growth to generate the jobs. Indeed, post-1994 growth data reveals that the only years in which the number and proportion of unemployed people declined were 2004-2007, when the economy grew at more than 5% of GDP.[36]

One reason for the high rates of unemployment is that the structure of the economy has changed significantly over the past six decades. In 1951 mining and agriculture contributed 28.7% to GDP, and financial services just 9.3%. In 2010, however, mining and agriculture contributed just 12.1%, and financial services 21.3%.[37] Therefore, the economy is moving towards relatively high-tech industries and high-skilled professions.

At the same time, private investment is playing an increasingly important role in generating GDP. In the 1980s private investors contributed between 50% and 60% of all fixed investment in South Africa. By the mid-2000s, as the government focused on social expenditure, and the political transition opened South Africa to new investors, the private sector was contributing more than 70% of fixed investment, peaking at

74% in 2006.[38] This figure has subsequently declined on the back of the global financial crisis, investor uncertainty, and new state infrastructure programmes.

The trend towards a more skilled and private sector-led market economy runs counter to some policy positions adopted by the government and the ANC. In chapter 5, I explained how policy initiatives such as GEAR and AsgiSA favoured a more prominent role for private sector investors, but provoked opposition from some elements within the tripartite alliance. Other policy initiatives, such as resolutions adopted at the ANC's National Conference in Polokwane in 2007, as well as the New Growth Path of 2011, favour greater state intervention in the economy, including a more active role in regulating the activities of the private sector.

This focus on state-centric economic development by some factions in the tripartite alliance has provoked considerable concern in the business and investment community. In July 2011 the chairman of Merrill Lynch, Humphrey Borkum, was quoted as saying: 'In my opinion, almost every company on the JSE is more efficient and competitive than any of our parastatals. If these parastatals were privatised, the taxes they would pay would result in more money for better housing, schools, and hospitals for the poor. At present they are a drag on the fiscus, and it is the small base of taxpayers that have to pay for all the inefficiency.'[39]

Not only the private sector is raising concerns about the state's ability to run businesses and create an environment in which privately owned businesses can flourish. In February 2012, the National Treasury stated that 'state-owned

enterprises need to change their investment planning framework from one that is based on what their balance sheet
can afford to one that is based on ascertaining what investments are required to unlock growth'.[40] In January 2013 the
director of the Centre for Development and Enterprise, Ann
Bernstein, argued in a research report that government policy
choices, with reference to labour market policy, were actually
destroying jobs in South Africa.[41]

In some cases, sheer incompetence is to blame for South
Africa's difficult and at times hostile business and investment environment. In August of 2013, for example, about
half of Johannesburg was left without electrical power after
a labour dispute within the local city council. It took three
days for the mayor to surface and make a statement, and four
days to restore the electricity supply. Among other things, the
Houghton home of a frail Nelson Mandela was left without
power, and an emergency generator had to be installed.

During that week I conducted a strategy session for a
European embassy on the future of the South African economy.
As usual, I argued that the ANC could introduce dramatic
reforms that would create a far better investment environment.
However, I struggled for answers when confronted with the
argument that, if this was the case, the ANC government could
surely be expected to keep the lights burning in the country's
economic heartland.

Corruption has contributed further to poor management
of the state's ventures into the business arena, and the hostile
business environment that too often prevails. Indeed, levels
of proven corruption have risen steadily in recent years. In an

autobiography published in 2008, the former DA leader Tony Leon recalled how his party had homed in on the 'wildfire spread of corruption under Mbeki', which he described as 'a growing mountain of sleaze'.[42] His reminiscences date back to the 1990s and early 2000s. A decade later, the public protector, Thuli Madonsela, described corruption as 'endemic', adding that the extent of the corruption she was encountering in the course of her work had the potential to 'distort the economy and derail democracy'.[43] And in 2012, the Institute for Democracy in South Africa (IDASA) reported that levels of corruption had reached their highest point since 1994.[44]

Social trends

Trends in the economic environment determine a number of trends in the social environment, ranging from inequality to calls for radical policy reforms. At the same time, trends in the social environment determine the views and attitudes of members of the public, and therefore the political pressures brought to bear on economic policy-makers. An analysis of those social trends, and the pressures that flow from them, follows below.

The high levels of inequality in the country were outlined in chapter 4. To a great extent this has been caused by failures in the public education system – which in turn leads to failures in the labour market. In 2010, there were just more than 1 million pupils in grade 10.[45] However, two years later, when they became the matric class of 2012, that number had fallen to just 511 000. In other words, almost half the pupils in grade 10 had failed to progress to grade 12. Moreover, only 377 829, or just over a third, passed their school-leaving exams. This is a trend we have identified every year for more than a decade – namely that only about half of learners get to matric, and only a third actually pass matric.

This is despite the fact that the pass mark has been reduced to aggregates of only 30%-40% (depending on the subject). In 2012, only 136 047 pupils, or just more than a tenth of those who had been in grade 10 in 2010, passed matric well enough to be admitted to university. However, caution is again warranted in respect of this figure as the minimum university admission mark has been reduced to matric aggregates of 40%-50% (again, depending on the subject). In 2012, only a quarter of the original 2010 cohort took mathematics as a subject in their final year at school, and just over 50 000 – or 5% – of the original 2010 grade 10 class passed mathematics with 50% or more.

Race was an important determinant of achievement in education. In 2010, for example, some 57% of whites aged 20-24 were enrolled in higher education, as opposed to 14% of blacks.[46] In 2012, while there were 851 000 whites in South Africa with a tertiary qualification, there were only 992 000 blacks with such a qualification. As a proportion of the population older than 20, this works out to 25% of whites as opposed to just 4% of blacks.[47]

Inequalities in education have implications for employment equity. For example, in 2012, 32% of top managers and 39% of senior managers were black.[48] These figures were a significant improvement on those of a decade earlier. In 2000 only 12.7% of top managers and 18.5% of senior managers were black. Yet, given that whites account for a tenth of the population, these figures still indicate high levels of social inequality.

High levels of poverty and inequality may explain negative public sentiment about the country's future, as well as the rise of radical sentiment captured in a number of South African opinion polls. In 2000, 72% of South Africans believed 'the government was performing well'. However, that figure had fallen to just below 50% by 2011 before recovering to 54% in 2012.[49] Similarly, the proportion of people who were confident of a 'happy future for all races' fell from 74% to 67% over a similar period,[50] the proportion who believed that 'race relations were improving' fell from 74% to 46%, and the proportion who believed South Africa was 'moving in the right direction' fell from a peak of 69% in 2006 to 46% in 2012.[51]

In 2011, only 41% of South Africans were satisfied with services provided by the government.[52] This figure was the lowest among blacks, at 38%.[53] Also, only 38% of people aged 18-24 were satisfied with government services, opposed to 50% of people aged 60 and older. Poorer people were also less satisfied than wealthier people; for example, while 46% of people in Living Standards Measure category 10 (LSM 10) were satisfied with service delivery, in LSM 1 that figure was a startling 0%.[54]

One of the risks related to an environment marked by high rates of unemployment, low rates of economic growth, and poor education is that it may serve as a breeding ground for radical sentiment. The rise of Julius Malema, the former ANC Youth League leader who has now started his own political movement, suggests that this risk must be taken seriously – which the

IRR has long maintained, even well before Malema became a household name. Malema promotes a brand of radical politics that, among other things, calls for the nationalisation of the mining industry. On a number of occasions, he has branded white South Africans as 'criminals' who must be treated as such.[55] In an opinion poll conducted in 2011, no less than 29% of adults said they supported what Malema said and did.[56] While this is admittedly a minority, 29% of adults are nonetheless a very large number of people. Similarly, an earlier opinion poll in 2011 found that 28% of urban adults believed the mines should be nationalised,[57] and a third poll found that 24% of blacks did not believe Malema's chanting of 'Kill the Boer, kill the farmer' at political rallies constituted hate speech.[58]

Rising negative sentiment may also explain why a number of civil society and media actors have been particularly active in holding the government to account over issues such as corruption, failed education, or adherence to the constitution. There are almost daily examples of civil society actors taking the government to court on a range of constitutional matters – and often winning.

At times, the government and the ANC have seemed increasingly annoyed by these challenges. In 2012, Zuma told parliament that the judiciary should 'stay out of policy matters',[59] and in 2011 the SACP accused judges of running a 'judicial dictatorship'.[60] Therefore there is a trend that at least some people in government and the ruling party are bent on undermining important feedback into the political system. In addition to threats against the judiciary there are threats to restrict access to official information via legislation such as the Protection of State Information Bill, as well as proposals for a media tribunal with powers to discipline journalists.[61]

The trends of greater civil society activism, and government threats to undermine such activism, as well as access to information, are likely to become increasingly prominent in any future system. Depending on which side prevails, the consequences for our final scenarios will be considerable.

To a certain extent, any government attempts to prevent feedback from discontented individuals or groups from entering the political arena of the country will probably be undone by the rise of communications technology and social media. The ability of citizens to exert popular pressure on the government is greatly increased by their access to technology, and especially information technology and the media.

For example, due to a successful roll-out of electricity, the great majority of South Africans now have access to independent means of receiving and disseminating information and ideas. The proportion of households without electricity has fallen from just under 50% in 1995 to 26% in 2012.[62] This has allowed the rapid uptake of mobile communications technology, even in poor communities.

An astonishing figure is the number of active cell phones in South Africa. This number has increased from 8.3 million in 2000 to over 68 million by 2013 – just imagine what a set of information-technology-related scenarios will show us about the next ten years.[63] The number of cell phones per 100 people in South Africa has increased from under 20 in 2000 to over 100 a decade later.[64]

This means that a big proportion of South Africans now have cellular phones, and thereby the means to communicate and disseminate their political demands via social media. Their experience of South Africa can therefore come to determine the dominant ideas within the country.

Despite many of them being poor and unemployed, thanks to mobile communication they probably have a better and greater ability to demand changes to the country than previous generations did.

Given the rise in negative and radical sentiments described earlier in this chapter, this trend will have many significant implications for our eventual scenarios.

As demonstrated by the recent uprisings in North Africa and the Middle East, cellular communications networks are also playing an increasingly important role in mass public protest. In fact, South Africa has higher levels of access to cellular phones than Egypt and Tunisia and a marginally lower level than Libya, three countries that recently underwent a period of rapid political destabilisation and change. In 2012 South Africa averaged 135 cellular phones per 100 people, while Libya averaged 148, Egypt 115, and Tunisia 120.[65] The impact this trend will have on our lives and our future cannot be emphasised enough.

Besides this, access to media such as television and radio has also increased very rapidly.[66] In the case of television, the proportion of households with a television set increased from 59% in 2002 to 89% in 2010. The rapid increase in the number of households during this period makes this figure all the more significant. The proportion of households with radios was 91.4%.

Probably the most important social trend is that the living standards of South Africans have improved significantly since 1994. From 2001 to 2010, there has been an absolute reduction in the number of people in the lower LSM categories, and an increase in the higher categories.[67] For example, the number of people in LSM 1 decreased from just over 3 million in 2001 to 1 million in 2012, while the proportion of South Africans in this category declined from almost 10% to less than 2%. Net declines were recorded for LSM 2 and 3 as well, leading to increases in LSMs 4 to 10. Thus we again see how the standard of living of most people has improved considerably over the past decade.

This may explain the ANC's continued electoral majorities. However, as I have pointed out, improved living standards are typically accompanied by increased expectations and may result in opinions turning against the government responsible for those improvements. This is especially so if levels of economic growth and educational standards remain as low as they are, meaning that individual actors have limited means to further improve their standards of living, and remain dependent on the state.

In our case, these improvements in living standards are largely due to rapid increases in access to basic services and welfare. Demand for such services has escalated quickly, despite relatively slow population growth of just on 1% a year.[68] The reason for this is that, despite the population increasing from 40.6 million in 1996 to 50.6 million in 2011 (or by 24%), the number of households increased from 9.1 million to 14.4 million, or by 58%, over the same period.[69] This, in turn, was due to a marked decline in average household size after the political transition.

Despite this increase in demand, households have gained significantly greater access to all types of services. For example, since 1996, the proportion of households using electricity for cooking increased from 47% to 71%, and those living in formal houses increased from 64% to 77%. This happened despite growing pressure on the state to deliver. This pressure is also partly caused by rapid rates of urbanisation over the past two decades. From 1990 to 2010, the proportion of South Africans living in urban areas increased from 52% to 62%.[70] Remarkably, despite an increase of more than 5 million households, and rising levels of urbanisation, the proportion of households living in shacks declined from 16% to 13% between 1996 and 2012.[71]

Equally important in meeting people's demands has been the roll-out of the government's social welfare programme. The number of people receiving social welfare increased from 2.9 million in 1996 to 16.6 million in 2013.[72] By 2010 welfare payments were reaching a third of the population, and there were almost three recipients of welfare for every taxpayer. Research shows that, whereas in 1994 more than three people were employed for every person on welfare, today more people are on welfare than are working.

As in the case of government-led service delivery, welfare has improved living standards. However, as with service delivery these living conditions improvements came at the cost of dependency. All of this helps to explain why the ANC has remained firmly ensconced in power even as it faces growing anger and criticism from its supporters.

Even though it reduces the worst aspects of poverty, welfare is now perhaps more of a threat than an asset to the ruling party. The budget deficit (the difference between government expenditure and revenue) is so great that the government will struggle to continue increasing the value of social grants.[73] Therefore, if inflation takes off once again, it will reduce the real living standards of families in South Africa that are dependent on welfare. The government will not be able to help these families, who in turn will blame the government for their declining living standards. This risk is so great that it could bring down the government. We will refer to this as the welfare or inflation trap in our eventual scenarios.

However, improvements in living standards have not solely resulted from state-led delivery and welfare. To a lesser extent, it has also resulted from the emergence of a small black middle class, which, in numerical terms, is beginning to approach the size of the white middle class. For example, in 2011, 27% of all bonds, houses, listed shares, money market holdings, and non-residential property were held by Africans, 5% by coloured people, 4% by Indian people, 41% by whites, and the balance by foreigners and the state. In 2010, 17.4% of shares listed on the JSE were owned by Africans, 3% by coloured people, 2.5% by Indians, 44.5% by whites, and the balance of 32.6% by foreigners and the state.[74] The share held by whites had fallen from 71.4%, as the shares held by blacks and foreigners rose.

Yet, the black middle class is a first-generation middle class and therefore differs greatly from the long-established white middle class. In addition, despite its relative growth, only 5%-7% of black South Africans as opposed to about 70% of white South Africans fall within our definition of middle class.[75] As a social trend, the size and importance of the black middle class, while important, is therefore generally overstated.

Making order out of chaos

As we work our way through these major political, economic, and social trends, a puzzling picture emerges of a country that is better off in many respects but that nonetheless underperforms on many key indicators. The ANC remains politically dominant, but is weakening at the same time. The party has delivered to millions of people but these same people also feel the party has betrayed them. Living standards have improved without jobs being created, and despite the weak performance of the economy. Regardless of service delivery successes and the roll-out of a massive state welfare programme, public opinion is turning against the government. Even though life in South Africa is undoubtedly better than in 1994, anti-government protests have taken off. For almost every point, there seems to be a counterpoint.

At the Centre for Risk Analysis we often warn our clients that – for a while, at least – they are likely to be more confused and uncertain about South Africa after meeting us than before. This is not necessarily a bad state of mind to be in when you begin a scenario planning exercise, as the real world is chaotic and confusing. It is impossible, other than by ignoring contradictory information and oversimplifying trends, to make easy sense of the trends we need to use to build our scenarios.

Do not be alarmed if you too are slightly puzzled by all the information presented in this chapter. Our next scenario step will be to start refining this information into a clear and concise set of major trends or key driving forces, which will lead us into the future.

HIGHWAYS
TO THE FUTURE

★ ★ ★

Consider presenting a university politics class with all the information we gathered in the previous chapters, and asking them to extrapolate what South Africa will look like in ten years' time. A confusing assortment of answers would emerge, because there is simply too much information for any individual to convert into a clearly articulated future.

The only way to make sense of such a wealth of information is to start grouping related pieces of data into what scenario planners commonly call key driving forces. These driving forces, and the various ways in which they can play out, will provide us with our highways to the future.

What have we found so far?

In the **political environment** we found that:

- The ANC is sustaining a significant majority in national elections.

- Except for the DA, opposition parties are becoming increasingly marginalised.
- A growing proportion of potential voters are staying away from the polls.
- Public protests against the quality of governance are growing.
- The ANC is deeply divided, and infighting in the party and the tripartite alliance is worsening.
- Aspects of the ANC's underlying ideology are at odds with the South African constitution.
- The ANC is increasingly hostile to the independence of the media and the judiciary.

In the **economic environment,** we found that:

- The South African economy is growing far more slowly than those of other emerging markets.
- Economic growth is constrained by poor savings and investment levels, low skills levels, and inadequate infrastructure.
- State revenue is constrained by a small tax base, and a large budget deficit poses a threat to future state expenditure.
- The economy is failing to create jobs for work-seekers, notably young people seeking to enter the labour market.
- Economic activity is increasingly moving to the tertiary sector, and is largely driven by private investment.
- Some policy-makers favour an open market economy, while others favour a state-controlled economy.

- Living standards of the majority of people have improved over the past decade, largely due to government welfare in the form of social grants and free or subsidised services.
- Higher rates of inflation could quickly erode the value of the state's extensive social grants programme.
- Blacks are playing a growing role in economic ownership and management. While the middle class is still largely made up of whites, it is becoming increasingly non-racial.

In the **social environment,** we found that:

- South African society is still highly unequal, largely along racial lines. Much of this is due to poor-quality education.
- Members of the public are increasingly critical about the government's performance and the state of the country.
- A third of South African adults support the radical – and often racist – views of extremist political leaders.
- Social actors and the media are successfully challenging the state in the public arena as well as in the courts.
- The state is seeking to curtail the extent to which people are able to use mechanisms such as the courts and the media to challenge its policies and actions.
- Widespread access to cellular networks allows people to communicate with one another and to access and disseminate information and ideas freely and quickly.

This amounts to 22 factors and trends, many of which run in different and sometimes contradictory directions.[1] Such a collection of trends simply involves too many variables to incorporate into a single analysis. This is why our politics class would have such a hard time using this information, as it stands, to describe a future South Africa.

We can make their task a lot easier by combining all these factors and trends into a smaller number of key driving forces. These driving forces ultimately shape the scenarios that await us just over the horizon. In this way, they can be said to provide us with highways to the future. While they all start in the present, these highways will gradually split and turn away along different routes towards each of the different futures, combining with the other highways along the way. Five such highways are particularly prominent:

Highway 1: The future of the ruling party

Numerous factors and trends identified in chapter 5, and above, relate to the internal and external strength of the ruling party and the threats it faces from opposition parties, voter desertion, radical opinions, and popular protests. These are listed in the table below:

Factors and trends pointing to the future of the ruling party
The ANC continues to win national elections with a comfortable majority.
While the DA is growing, all the other opposition parties are declining.

More and more potential voters are choosing not to participate in the formal electoral system.

Violent public protests against the quality of governance are increasing.

The ANC is increasingly divided, and infighting within the party is becoming increasingly severe.

South Africa remains a highly unequal society, largely along racial lines.

Public opinion about the quality of governance as well as national progress is becoming increasingly negative.

A third of South African adults support the radical beliefs of extremist political leaders.

Access to cellular communications allows people to disseminate information freely and quickly.

Taken together, they point to a single driving force – the future of the ruling party – that will have a major impact on South Africa's future. This is an example of a driving force whose outcome is very uncertain, which makes it highly relevant to our eventual scenarios. At the one extreme, the tripartite alliance will remain intact and consolidate its political control. At the other, the alliance may disintegrate and lose political control over the country.

Let us consider some of the implications. For example, in order to remain in power, the ANC government might introduce drastic economic, labour market and education reforms, and South Africa could become more prosperous. Alternatively, the ANC government might seek to contain protest and dissent by curtailing democratic institutions and practices. In this case, the government would become increasingly authoritarian. A third possibility is that, should the ANC fail to introduce successful reforms, or fail to weaken demand mechanisms, it could lose an election or be driven from power by increasingly radical populist movements. Clearly, this highway, and its possible destinations, will have a major bearing on our route to the future.

Highway 2: Citizens' ability to change the government

A second key driving force offering us a highway to the future is the extent to which citizens will retain the means to change the government. This must be weighed against the risk that the government might seek to restrict the ability of people do this. This highway emerges from the following factors and trends:

Factors and trends pointing to citizens' ability to change the government
The ANC's underlying ideology seems at odds with the constitution, and therefore the agreed values governing the current political system.
Social actors and the media are successfully challenging the state.

The state is seeking to curtail the extent to which social actors can access feedback mechanisms in order to challenge the state.

Access to cellular networks allows people to communicate and to disseminate information freely and quickly.

Again, this highway can swing in two very different directions. At the one extreme, individual, political, economic, and social actors could use the courts, the media, and the electoral system to insist that the government meets their demands. At the other, access to these mechanisms could be eroded to such an extent that the government could rule with impunity.

Consider the implications for the future. If people retain the ability to hold the government to account or to remove it from power, the political costs of poor economic policy and poor economic performance could be very high, forcing the government to introduce meaningful reforms. If it fails to do so, or if its reforms fail to achieve the desired result, the ANC might be removed from power.

Alternatively, the government might seek to pre-empt such a defeat by curtailing freedoms such as access to the courts, the media, and civil society. In this case, it will not matter whether citizens' demands are met, because they would be powerless to remove the current government. This begins to show us how identifying numerous highways helps us to gain insight into what our future holds.

Highway 3: The future of the South African economy

A third highway relates to the future growth of the South African economy. It emerges from the trends listed below:

Factors and trends pointing to the future of the economy
The South African economy is growing far more slowly than those of other emerging markets.
The economy is constrained by a number of structural factors, including low investment and savings rates, a persistent current account deficit, low skills levels, and inadequate infrastructure.
Revenue collection is constrained by a small tax base.
The economy has been unable to meet demands for employment.
Access to good-quality education is limited.
A minority of white South Africans dominates economic activity.
The poor education of many youths limits their potential for employment and heightens their demands on the system.

Again, this highway could head in two very different directions. At the one extreme, South Africa builds a well-managed market economy that grows rapidly enough to absorb new job-seekers and reduce the unemployment backlog. Living standards are improved, and inequality is reduced. Tax revenue rises, which allows the government to reduce its debt levels, improve vital public services such as health and education, and improve the country's infrastructure, thus stimulating further economic growth. At the other extreme, poor policy choices – including attempts at state intervention – continue to hamper economic growth, thus worsening unemployment, poverty, and inequality.

Again, it is instructive to start considering some of the turns this highway could take. Should the economy grow rapidly enough to reduce unemployment, it might begin to reduce the very high levels of inequality that are posing a growing risk to political stability. The ANC might regain its popularity, even winning new supporters in the middle classes. This would provide a platform for consolidating democracy and entrenching civil liberties, which would help to boost investor confidence and therefore add to the virtuous circle of economic growth.

Conversely, should growth and investment remain at current levels, rising levels of poverty and inequality could fuel popular dissatisfaction, to the point where most citizens completely want to change the way in which the country is governed. In this case, an increasingly beleaguered government might seek to curtail rising pressures by diminishing civil liberties, while blaming continued poverty and inequality on the private sector and the largely white middle class.

Highway 4: The capacity of the state to continue providing social welfare

A fourth highway involves the capacity of the state to maintain its current welfare programme in the form of social grants as well as free or subsidised services such as housing, water, and electricity. Whether we like it or not, we have to accept that a large proportion of the population may depend on state welfare for the rest of their lives, regardless of future economic performance. This highway emerges from the following trends:

Factors and trends pointing to the capacity of the state to continue providing social welfare
State revenue is constrained by a small tax base.
South Africa's social system is marked by significant race-based inequalities.
Living standards have improved considerably over the past decade, largely due to state welfare in the form of social grants and free or subsidised services.
Welfare has reduced the worst effects of poverty. Welfare payments now reach a third of the population.

Again, this highway could take some very different turns. At the one extreme, higher levels of economic growth enable the state to maintain its welfare programme, thus sustaining the living standards of a third of the population. At the other, the state is overwhelmed by popular demands, with far-reaching consequences. Should the state retain its capacity to meet current demand, as well as rising expectations for welfare and service delivery, this would help to stabilise the social order. However, should demands and expectations begin to outstrip the state's capacity to deliver, South Africa could destabilise in a matter of months.

Consider, for example, the implications of a few years of increasingly poor tax collection while the government maintains an already unsustainable budget deficit. Consider what would happen if the global economy were to recover and a large chunk of the taxpaying middle classes emigrates. Or think of the impact of a few months of high food price inflation on the living standards of poor households. Combined with other factors and trends – such as the maintenance of a free and open society – this driving force could introduce huge shifts in our future. Imagine what the consequences may be of a rapid drop in the real value of social grants in a country whose citizens could remove the government from power in a single voting day.

Does this seem unlikely? Well, that is what analysts thought for decades about regimes ranging from the former Soviet Union to Egypt, which were toppled despite being far more strongly entrenched – in far less democratic systems – than the ANC.

Highway 5: Economic policy

The fifth and final highway is future economic policy. This is probably the most important highway in the sense that it is likely to have the greatest impact on our future and is also highly uncertain. It emerges from the following factors and trends:

Factors and trends pointing to economic policy

The economy is increasingly centred on the tertiary sector, and is primarily driven by private investment.

Most policy-makers support increased state intervention in the economy, while others support a private sector-led growth model.

Again, this highway could swing in very different directions, ranging from a deregulated market economy to a heavily regulated, state-managed economy. These two extremes will create very different futures. A state-led development model, marked by corruption and inefficiency, would fail to deliver the levels of growth needed to improve national prosperity. A deregulated market economy, which attracts new investment and encourages entrepreneurial talent, would achieve higher levels of GDP growth, thus creating jobs and improving living standards.

The state-led economic model would involve more business regulation, even higher levels of worker protection, and more onerous BEE and affirmative action codes. The government would attempt to restrict imports and protect the domestic economy by raising tariff barriers. State corporations would be active in numerous economic sectors, including mining, agriculture, banking and finance. The labour market would be more strictly regulated, and property rights would be eroded.

The private sector-led growth model would be very different. BEE and affirmative action requirements and labour laws would be watered down. Import tariffs would be reduced or abolished, as companies learn to compete in the global economy. Property rights would be guaranteed, thus helping to restore investor confidence and raise investment levels. Higher levels of international and domestic investment would encourage entrepreneurship and drive higher levels of growth, which would create jobs, reduce poverty and inequality, and therefore improve living standards. People would take charge of their own welfare, thus reducing the welfare burden on the state. The state would be left to attend to its main duties such as providing defence, law and order, and decent infrastructure.

The process of defining these highways begins to demonstrate the value of the scenario method adopted in this book. It has allowed us to reduce the state of South Africa to just 22 factors and trends, and these into just five key driving forces that act as highways to the future. There is no other method that would have allowed us to identify such a wide range of political, economic and social factors and trends, and combine them into such a small set of drivers with such a defining influence over the future.

Just think of how much simpler the task we set our university class has now become. The students will be presented with this set of highways and must argue how they will interact and combine with one another in order to describe our future. For example, they might state that on **highway 1** the ANC will retain political control of South Africa. This will be because on **highway 2** the ANC government has successfully limited the capacity of citizens to hold it to account. This will be because on **highway 3** the economy performs very poorly, and the ANC fears losing a future election. This will be because on **highway 4** the party understands that poor economic performance threatens its capacity to continue delivering social welfare. And all of this occurs because on **highway 5** the party takes the wrong economic policy decisions. In this instance, the student would have produced a clear description of a future involving a closed and undemocratic political system with a failing economy.

Road signs along our highways to the future

A key question is this: How do we know in which direction our highways are turning? Fortunately, there are a number of road signs that will line the route we will be taking into the future. Identifying these is the seventh step in our scenario building exercise.

Road signs along
★　★　★　**HIGHWAY 1**　★　★　★
The future of the ruling party

The first significant road sign along this highway to the future is *electoral outcomes*. This is an obvious indicator, but a valuable one. If the ANC manages to reverse the current trend of declining popularity and strengthen its support at the polls, we can be almost certain that the tripartite alliance will retain political control of South Africa. However, if the ANC's share of the vote drops below 60%, we can be almost certain that the party is on the way to losing the 2024 election, and we are heading for a period of far-reaching change.

The second road sign is the *results of opinion polls*. Many political opinion polls are conducted in South Africa. Those utilised by the DA are regarded as particularly effective, producing accurate predictions of election outcomes. A DA member of parliament recently told me that the party usually knows the outcome of an election 'within 1 percentage point' before any votes have been cast. This data is not in the public domain, but a lot of other data is. If these show that public opinion is turning against the ANC government, this would be a marker on the road to an ANC defeat at the polls. If polls reveal the opposite, we are probably heading towards another scenario.

A third road sign is the *extent of public protests*. If public protests decline, this would point towards the tripartite alliance retaining political control up to the 2024 elections. However, if violent protests continue to escalate, this points to a scenario in which the ANC government is likely to lose power.

A fourth road sign is *levels of conflict within the tripartite alliance*. The ANC is supported by an alliance with the SACP and COSATU, which is riven by mounting internal conflict. An alliance at odds with itself will never be able to play an effective role in governing South Africa. As long as alliance members differ among themselves about issues as serious as the nationalisation of the mines, the government will remain paralysed, and unable to meet popular expectations. Should the alliance develop a new consensus on key policy issues, this could open the door to more effective government policy, which could consolidate the ANC's hold on power. By contrast, should conflict within the alliance continue or escalate further, it would increasingly detract from the ANC's ability to govern, thus adding to threats to its power. Should the alliance break up, this would effectively end the ANC's monopoly on the popular vote, and propel party politics into a new and more fluid phase in which the ANC is likely to lose votes to opposition parties.

Related to this, the fifth road sign is the *ANC's relationship with COSATU and the SACP*. Should the ANC move to marginalise both groupings and replace their leaders with more pliant figures (as it did with the ANC Youth League), this would show that it intends to introduce some market-friendly policy reforms. However, if more SACP and COSATU hardliners are given top government jobs, this would be a sign that economic reform is unlikely.

Road signs along
★ ★ ★ **HIGHWAY 2** ★ ★ ★
Citizens' ability to change the government

The first road sign along this highway is the *independence of the electoral system*, as administered by the Electoral Commission of South Africa, popularly known as the Independent Electoral Commission (IEC). Should the government begin to tamper with the IEC's autonomy, this may be a sign that it wants to start manipulating the results of future elections. As our Zimbabwean neighbours have come to learn, when this happens, it does not matter how unpopular the government becomes, since there are no democratic means of removing it from power. However, if the IEC's independence is maintained, we are likely to remain on a route where popular opinion determines South Africa's future direction.

The second road sign along this highway is the *ability of citizens to access information and circulate ideas*. Ideas are very powerful; they determine people's actions, as well as government policy. For example, the apartheid government was based on the notion of racial separation, reflected in a range of laws and regulations – from the Group Areas Act to job reservation and the pass laws. These policies only changed when NP leaders started to abandon the idea of racial separation. Today, a dominant idea shared by the government and the opposition is that of redress and redistribution, reflected in policies ranging from land reform to BEE. As long as people retain access to information about trends and events in their society, and the ability to articulate their ideas, they are able to change the dominant ideas in that society, and hence its policies. Conversely, if access to information and the right to air ideas is restricted, room for shifts in ideas – and therefore shifts in a country's future – is more limited.

The third road sign along this highway is the *independence of the media*. Free and vigorous media keep the government on its toes. The media play a major role in shaping beliefs and ideas, and can play a central role in changing South Africa's future. However, when the freedom of the media is curtailed, they become less effective as agents of change.

The fourth road sign is the *standing of civil society*. This is very similar to the status of the media. Well-resourced and independent advocacy and research groups can do a great deal to capture the public imagination and change the country's future. The success of the Treatment Action Campaign (TAC) in forcing the government to change its policies on HIV and AIDS is a notable example. However, when the government starts to take steps to curtail the fundraising, registration, and operation of civil society organisations, people lose an important means of changing the future.

Road signs along

★ ★ ★ **HIGHWAY 3** ★ ★ ★

The future of the South African economy

The first road sign along this highway is *economic growth*. This is relatively obvious. Should South Africa achieve a sustained growth rate of more than 5% of GDP, this would indicate a better future. Should economic growth continue to languish at rates lower than 3%, this would lead us towards a bleaker future.

The second road sign is *investment and savings levels*, expressed as proportions of GDP, and compared with those in other emerging markets. Investment levels show how much money international investors are prepared to commit to projects in South Africa, and, by extension, their confidence in its future. Higher levels of fixed investment would show that we are moving to the upper extreme of this driving force. Declining investment levels would show the opposite. Similarly, without raising our domestic savings level to 25% of GDP, we will not be able to raise levels of economic growth above 5% of GDP.

The third road sign is the *performance of the education*

system. We are increasingly moving towards a high-tech and high-skills economy. If our education system does not keep pace with this evolution, we will not be able to achieve and sustain growth of 5% of GDP or create job opportunities for young people. Relevant indicators are the number of matriculants passing maths with scores of 50% or higher, and the number of business and engineering graduates leaving our universities every year. These are obviously not the only skills needed by our economy, but they are a good benchmark of the standards and output of our education system.

The fourth road sign is the *state of the global economy*. This factor is largely out of our hands, but nevertheless has a significant impact on our economy and therefore the country's future. In times of global economic distress, our economy will be adversely affected, and, during periods of rapid global economic growth, our prospects may also improve.

I add this road sign with some reluctance as it is so often misused by South African policy-makers as an excuse for our poor economic performance. During the recent global financial crisis, a number of emerging markets managed to maintain far higher rates of economic growth than South Africa. Domestic policies play a far greater role in determining our economic prospects than the global environment.

The fifth road sign along this highway is South Africa's *current account deficit,* which could indicate that the country is falling into a debt trap. This could precipitate a flight of investors as well as a currency crash. Watch here for signs of disinvestment, foreign interest rate rises, and any populist move to lower interest rates by a considerable margin.

Road signs along

★ ★ ★ **HIGHWAY 4** ★ ★ ★

The capacity of the state to continue providing welfare

The first route markers along highway 4 are the *unemployment* and *labour market participation rates*. If these remain at or near current levels, they would point to the same or even greater levels of dependency on social welfare, combined with limited tax resources to meet those demands. Conversely, as more people start working and take charge of their own welfare, levels of dependence would decline even as tax revenue rose.

The second road sign would be the size of the *budget deficit*. The state budget determines the ability of the state to provide welfare in the form of social grants and free services. In a high-deficit environment, it would become increasingly difficult to sustain the extensive welfare programme. In order to do so, the government would have to cut investments in areas such as infrastructure and security. However, should the budget deficit be restricted to manageable levels, especially in a context of high levels of economic growth, the welfare programme should remain affordable.

The third is the *rate of inflation*. As inflation rises, it reduces the real standard of living of poor households. This is the 'inflation/welfare trap' referred to previously, and a vital road sign along this highway. Should inflation rise significantly, the government would not be able to afford the increases in welfare spend necessary to sustain the living standards of poor people. If this happens, and the current living standards of poor people begin to fall, we can expect some dramatic changes.

The fourth is the *level of public protests*. This reflects the extent to which people are dissatisfied with the government's performance.

Road signs along
★ ★ ★ **HIGHWAY 5** ★ ★ ★
Economic policy

The first road sign along this highway relates to *BEE and affirmative action*. If these laws and regulations are softened or repealed, this will show the government is so desperate to achieve higher levels of economic growth that it will do almost anything to improve economic performance. Some cynics will say this will never happen. They should be careful about this kind of prediction. Go back to the night of 15 August 1988 and the Rubicon speech, when PW Botha promised the country and the world that the NP would never relinquish its principles. At that point, most analysts would have dismissed the notion that Nelson Mandela would be president within ten years as beyond the bounds of possibility.

Think too about the difficult position the ANC currently finds itself in. More and more voters are staying away from the polls, and protest levels are skyrocketing. Violence against the state is a daily occurrence. The budget deficit shows that the government is unable to raise the money it needs to implement its policies. It can only be saved by higher levels of economic growth, which will produce more jobs and more tax revenue.

Should the ANC believe it may lose an election, it may well decide to scale down BEE and affirmative action and their costs to the economy. In fact, it appears at times, at least if you read between the lines, that the ANC is thinking in this direction already. However, there is also a good chance that it may tighten up BEE requirements even further, in a desperate attempt to meet popular demands for a bigger share of the economic spoils. If BEE and affirmative action requirements are made even more onerous, this would show that we are moving towards increased state intervention in the economy.

The second road sign along this highway relates to *labour regulations*, with the same arguments applying here as in the case of BEE. The government desperately wants to create more jobs, and is afraid of the unemployed, who may turn on it. But its own labour laws are regularly cited as obstacles to job creation and economic growth. Should it begin to reduce the regulatory burden on employers, this could point towards a move to an open market economy and a private sector-led growth model. By contrast, should the government further tighten labour market regulations – which it is currently doing – this would point towards increased state control over the economy.

The third road sign relates to *trade protectionism and parastatals*. Here one indicator would be whether the government continues to bail out failing state-owned businesses and whether it establishes any new ones. Another indicator would be whether or not the government reduces or increases tariffs on imports. Should it cut or abolish tariffs, this will show that it expects the private sector to compete in a global economy. Should it raise tariffs, or introduce new ones, this will show that it is seeking to protect uncompetitive state-led industries, and favours higher levels of state control of the economy.

The fourth road sign relates to the *public role of the business community*. There is a large gap between what business leaders say in the privacy of their boardrooms, and what they say in public. If business leaders continue to shrink back from publicly supporting their ideological friends and allies in the government, the policy environment can only get worse. In such a scenario, future economic policy will largely be shaped or influenced by left-leaning politicians and journalists, civil society groupings, and trade unions. However, if business leaders throw their considerable weight (and financial muscle) behind good policy proposals, and the people in government who support them, economic policies are more likely to improve.

Building a scenario matrix

We are now familiar with the highways that will carry us to the future. We have also identified many of the road signs that will line those highways and give us a sense of the direction we are moving in. But we still do not know what the final destinations we could be travelling towards look like.

This takes us to step 8 of our scenario building exercise, namely to select two driving forces and use these as the two axes of a scenario matrix, from which our final scenarios – and therefore our final destinations – will emerge.

Scenario planners usually select the two most important and most uncertain driving forces – in other words, the ones that would have the biggest impact, and whose outcomes

145

are most unpredictable. However, all the driving forces will eventually be brought into play, and experience has shown that the outcomes will be more or less the same regardless of which driving forces are chosen as the axes for the scenario matrix.

In my view, South Africans' ability to change the government is the most important of our five driving forces and will have the greatest impact on the future. It could produce highly divergent outcomes, ranging from one in which South Africans could change their government relatively easily, to one where the government could rule with impunity. Given continued access to elections, the media, and civil society, the actions of ordinary South Africans, in pursuit of better lives for themselves and their families, will shape the future to a greater extent than any other driving force. However, should access to demand mechanisms be constrained, citizens could do nothing to change the government even if it fails to meet their expectations. This driving force is therefore a good choice for the 'impact' axis of our scenario matrix.

The most uncertain driving force is future economic policy. Possible outcomes range from a situation where the private sector dominates the economy, to one where the state directs all economic activity. We know that elements of the tripartite alliance favour the nationalisation of industry and the mining sector. Others favour a market economy driven by private investment. The outcome is highly uncertain. The stance of the business sector on economic policy is also often confused. Organised business supports policies such as land reform and BEE, but complains that the regulatory environment is hostile, skills are in short supply, and property rights are uncertain. While they will not say this in public, many business leaders and senior managers believe current BEE policy is a major obstacle to investment in South Africa.

The DA's stance on economic policy is also unclear, and sometimes contradictory. While it supports a non-racial 'open opportunity' society on the one hand, it also professes to support BEE and affirmative action on the other. It has even supported legislation that promises jail time for investors who break BEE laws. With none of the tripartite alliance, the business community, or the opposition being clear on where they stand, future economic policy remains highly uncertain.

These two driving forces can now be used as the axes of a matrix, which appears on the following page. The horizontal axis represents the extent to which South Africans retain control of the means to change the government. The left side of the axis represents an environment in which access to feedback mechanisms, such as elections and the media, is increasingly restricted. The right side of the axis represents an environment in which most people have the means to express their needs and aspirations, and hold the government to account.

The vertical axis represents the different directions economic policy can take. The top end represents a free and open market economy, and the bottom end a heavily regulated and state-led economy.

The four quadrants of the matrix each contain the kernel of a plausible future, or the wire frame of a scenario. They are based on how the most important and most uncertain driving forces combine and play themselves out over the next decade.

These are the four destinations to which our highways to the future may lead us.

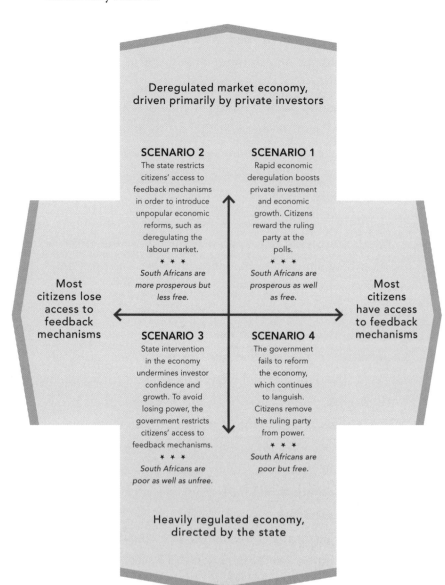

THE SCENARIO MATRIX

The selection of these two driving forces or highways as the axes of our scenario matrix does not mean we are jettisoning the others. Moreover, as noted previously, the eventual scenarios will also not differ much if we pick any other driving forces as the axes. All the other driving forces remain just as important, and will play themselves out in the various scenarios. These wire frames will be fleshed out into proper scenarios in the chapters that follow, but short descriptions follow:

Scenario 1: The government introduces economic reforms, but rides out popular dissent until the effects of higher levels of economic growth are felt by all, and feedback mechanisms remain accessible to a majority of actors in the system. South Africa becomes more prosperous while remaining a free society. I call this the 'Wide Road' scenario.

Scenario 2: The government introduces economic reforms, aimed at achieving higher levels of growth, which are unpopular with a large segment of the population. The government deals with this by curtailing access of citizens to feedback mechanisms – in other words, the ability of citizens to register their demands and aspirations and feed them back into the system. Economic prosperity is gained at the cost of personal freedom. This is the 'Narrow Road' scenario.

Scenario 3: The state plays an increasingly active role in managing the economy. In response to growing dissatisfaction with poor economic performance, it restricts citizens' access to feedback mechanisms in order to prevent critical feedback from entering the political system. South Africa becomes poorer, but citizens are unable to do anything about it. This is the 'Rocky Road' scenario.

Scenario 4: The state plays an increasingly active role in managing the economy. Economic growth lags, and the government is unable to quell rising levels of public protest and dissent. People use feedback mechanisms such as elections to force the ANC from power. South Africa is very poor and still unequal but, for the time being, its people are free to choose their government and the policies which govern them. I call this the 'Toll Road' scenario as the ANC stalls the economy through bad and unpopular policy decisions.

These four scenario logics cover all of South Africa's plausible futures. All four outcomes differ greatly from one another, and all of them depict a very different country from the one we know today. Several of these futures differ so drastically that there is no way in which current trends could have been used to forecast them. This is exactly what we want to achieve, as we know from experience, most recently from the North African uprisings, that countries can change very rapidly and in ways that few people anticipate.

Nothing can happen that is not accounted for within the boundaries of these four scenarios. Have no doubt, therefore, that your experience of South Africa in 2024 will reflect one of these four outcomes. As we proceed towards our target date, the road signs along our highways to the future will gradually begin to show us which of our four destinations is coming into view.

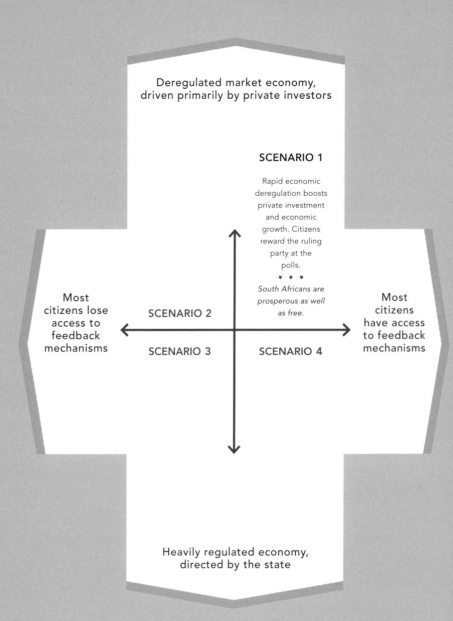

Deregulated market economy,
driven primarily by private investors

SCENARIO 1

Rapid economic
deregulation boosts
private investment
and economic
growth. Citizens
reward the ruling
party at the
polls.

* * *

*South Africans are
prosperous as well
as free.*

Most
citizens lose
access to
feedback
mechanisms

SCENARIO 2

SCENARIO 3   SCENARIO 4

Most
citizens
have access
to feedback
mechanisms

Heavily regulated economy,
directed by the state

In the Wide Road scenario the trend highways lead
us into a future where citizens are free and have become
more prosperous.

WIDE ROAD

(SCENARIO 1)[1]

It is May 2024. The ANC has just won another national election with a comfortable majority, and its current leader has been sworn in as president. South Africa is a free and open society. The economy is growing rapidly, and citizens are more prosperous and more content. This is a dramatic turnaround from the state of affairs ten years ago when governance was deteriorating, the economy was lagging, new radical political movements were threatening to destabilise the country, and analysts and observers were sounding dire warnings about its future.

After flirting with defeat at the polls, the ANC has rebuilt its support base. The party is more united and forward-looking, and has formed a more effective government. It has also abandoned its socialist and redistributionist leanings, which once threatened to strangle the economy. The judiciary, the media, and civil society are strong and independent.

The economy is growing at more than 5% a year, creating enough jobs to absorb new work-seekers and reduce the unemployment backlog. Economic reforms, ranging from the deregulation of labour markets to scaling down employment equity and BEE, have stimulated domestic and foreign investment. The savings rate has increased significantly, and foreign and domestic fixed investment rates now match those of leading emerging markets. The labour force participation rate has improved significantly, and income levels have increased.

This has improved the living standards of the vast majority of South Africans. Most importantly, these improvements have been brought about by economic growth, job creation, education, and entrepreneurship as much as by welfare and redistribution. Popular protests have died out, and opinion polls reveal that most South Africans are optimistic about the future.

How did we get here?

A decade ago, the ANC government was beset by a growing array of problems. Its standing and credibility were weakened by nepotism and corruption. Infighting was increasingly paralysing its ability to make or implement policy. Despite its relative success in delivering social welfare in the form of social grants and free services, opinion polls showed that South Africans were increasingly disillusioned with the ANC, and dissatisfied with the government's performance. International opinion was also rapidly turning against South Africa's previously lauded post-apartheid government. The optimism and sense of idealism surrounding post-apartheid South Africa had largely evaporated.

More and more analysts began to entertain an idea that had previously been unthinkable, namely that the ANC might lose power in the foreseeable future. The DA certainly believed this was possible, and stated that it was working towards unseating the ANC government by 2024. Some ANC insiders also warned that, unless something drastic was done, the movement would go into terminal decline.

Former supporters of the ANC in the media and civil society were also turning against the party. Many role players and opinion-formers in the media and civil society had welcomed the ANC's ascent to power. However, by 2014 that had begun to change. An increasingly activist media were regularly airing allegations of corruption and nepotism. Civil society organisations were routinely resorting to the courts and Chapter 9 institutions to force the government to investigate allegations of corruption, or improve services such as providing schools with desks, chairs, and textbooks.

The sense that the ANC was losing its grip on the country gathered momentum in the 2014 elections when the party's share of votes cast dropped for the third straight election. Low voter turnout figures for the party meant that it had captured the votes of just four out of every ten South Africans of voting age. However, it was this disappointing election result that finally galvanised a group of reformist ANC leaders into arresting the party's decline, and turning its fortunes around.

This group was led by key figures in the administration of former president Thabo Mbeki, and included ANC deputy president Cyril Ramaphosa, former finance minister Trevor Manuel, former labour minister and Reserve Bank governor Tito Mboweni, and Reserve Bank governor Gill Marcus. Spurred into action, they began to campaign aggressively, both within and outside the tripartite alliance, for a new party leadership that could refocus and reinvigorate the ANC, and save it from an inglorious demise.

This campaign was driven by two main insights. The first was that higher levels of economic growth were necessary to accelerate national development and meet the expectations of their supporters. The reformists understood that simply seeking to increase living standards via social welfare would continue to create popular expectations that could not be met, and drive up mass discontent. By contrast, the economy needed to create enough jobs to allow the majority of people to take charge of their own welfare and meet their own expectations of a better life.

Second, the reformist group understood that any efforts to undermine democratic institutions, in order to remain in power, and force through unpopular reforms could backfire. They recognised that civil society and the media were strong and active enough to ward off any such assault on civil liberties. Rather, they would need to work with those institutions in convincing citizens of the benefits of reform.

The reformists argued that the ANC was being held back by outdated doctrines, infighting, corruption and nepotism. They argued that a new generation of leaders with new ideas was required to unite the party and its supporters behind policies aimed at stimulating economic growth.

Their emergence provoked significant conflict within the tripartite alliance. On the one hand, their reformist message resonated with growing numbers of ANC leaders as well as members in the provinces and branches who were increasingly exposed to community dissatisfaction with the party and government. On the other, they were bitterly opposed by leaders who were entrenched in power and benefiting from nepotism and patronage, as well as radical elements that still believed that socialism and racial nationalism were viable ways forward.

Ironically, this conflict within the alliance was equated with the conflict between the *verligtes* (enlightened) and *verkramptes* (ultra-conservatives) in Afrikaner politics in the 1970s and 1980s. The *verligtes* recognised the need for drastic reforms, and a negotiated political settlement. The *verkramptes* believed the apartheid state could and should continue to hang on to power without making any economic and political concessions. Like their counterparts three decades earlier, the ANC's new *verligtes* skilfully isolated the new *verkramptes*, removing them from key leadership and decision-making processes in the party and government, and thereby gained policy control of the tripartite alliance. This in turn allowed them to introduce a series of significant policy reforms.

First, they reformed labour market policy by introducing youth wage subsidies, aimed at encouraging employers to hire more young people. They repealed the horizontal application of the collective bargaining system – which allowed large employers to strike wage hike deals with unions and then force small employers to implement the same wage hikes. This was a policy that had long been abused by large businesses to drive smaller competitors out of business. After the reforms, large established businesses could no longer hold smaller competitors under their thumb, and consequently small business activity took off. The reformers also watered down several provisions of the Labour Relations Act and the Basic Conditions of Employment Act, thus encouraging employers to hire more workers and become more internationally competitive.

Second, they restructured BEE and employment equity policies, abandoning punitive racial targets and quotas in favour of a more enabling framework that encouraged entrepreneurship, job creation and investment. The very idea of empowerment changed from one of ticking off boxes to meet race targets – to one that promoted investment and job creation.

Their third initiative was to reform the public schooling system, notably by curbing the power of teachers' unions to resist changes aimed at making teachers more accountable; giving parents and communities a greater role in managing schools; and encouraging competition among schools, among other things by introducing education vouchers that enabled parents to send their children to any school of their choice.

The fourth was to get the government out of business through the dispersal sale of parastatals, ranging from South African Airways to Transnet and Eskom. These entities were privatised, with the result that they became taxpayer as opposed to tax consumers, while providing far better services.

Their fifth initiative was to turn the broad policy thrust away from race and redistribution towards merit and economic growth. Cadre deployment was abandoned, and stricter and more effective measures introduced for combating corruption in the public sector. For example, government employees and members of their immediate families were prohibited from doing business with the government. Likewise, lifestyle audits were carried out across all government departments to identify and root out corrupt officials. The civil service became more professional and accountable, and government services began to improve.

Many of these policy shifts were strongly resisted by radical elements within the alliance, who argued that the new ANC leadership was selling out to whites and big business. Left-leaning civil society leaders and journalists, for example, saw the relaxation of labour laws as an affront to the human dignity of workers.

There were some tense public confrontations between the reformists and left-wing radicals who were organising into a new workers' movement to oppose the reforms. However, thanks to their controlling position in the ANC, the reformists were able to guide the alliance and government through these crises, providing them with convincing new public arguments for countering left-wing propaganda.

For example, when nurses and teachers went on strike in protest against labour reforms, key figures in the government and party were able to accuse them of betraying the public and undermining public health and education services. Likewise, when civil society sought to challenge some labour market reforms in the courts, the government argued successfully that special measures were necessary to reduce South Africa's extreme unemployment levels.

Ironically, the reform movement was strongly criticised by a vocal minority of members of the black middle class, through organisations such as the Black Management Forum. These organisations were the gatekeepers of BEE policy and their members had grown rich from inflated public, and private tenders and 'sweetheart' empowerment deals offered by large corporations. In response to such vocal criticism, the government adopted a dual strategy of placating this special interest group, while warning them that, without significantly faster economic growth, a revolution of the black poor was a real possibility. At times the government went as far as presenting the pro-BEE community as a greedy elite standing in the way of a more equal society. This was political grandstanding at its best – but it worked. Poor communities and ordinary ANC supporters, who had no chance of benefiting from BEE deals, came to accept the arguments against the policy and the need for policy reform.

The government therefore found that its arguments in favour of reform were effective across a range of interest groups. It won the support of most middle-class people, who understood that economic progress would stabilise the country. It was also supported by think-tanks and the business press. The business community, delighted that the government was finally 'leading' South Africa after years of intransigence on policy, loudly backed the line taken by the reform movement. Moreover, many poor people rallied behind the dominant reformist idea, namely that people should be given the opportunity to work, and not just depend on the state.

A new national consensus began to emerge, which moved away from the notion of state welfare and redistribution towards the idea that people should be empowered to work and start businesses, and thereby improve their own lives. This allowed the reformists to press ahead with far-reaching changes to the economic policy framework.

The government understood that these reforms needed to be underpinned by hard evidence that they were working. Fortunately, this was evident from early on in the reform process. Just a few years after the 2014 national elections, the economy was growing at 5% of GDP. This was almost twice the moving average of the two decades to 2014, and matched the average rate of growth of other BRICS countries. As a result, unemployment began to recede, dropping below 20% by the 2019 elections, and below 15% before the elections in 2024.

Higher levels of economic growth and job creation broadened the corporate and individual tax base and increased tax revenue, and the budget deficit dropped to 3% of GDP. Increased investment, economic deregulation, and improved productivity boosted exports, which brought the current account deficit under control.

The number of matric maths passes also increased rapidly as the education policy reforms took hold. By 2024 significantly more black than white engineers, doctors, and lawyers were set to graduate from South African universities.

Income levels increased across all social strata. These

improvements, and the associated improvements in living standards, had more to do with improved employment levels than with social welfare. For the first time, poor households could claim credit for improving their own circumstances. Service delivery protests waned as unemployment declined. Opinion polls reflected renewed confidence in the government and the ANC. This was reflected in election results that saw ANC support levels stabilise in the 2019 election, and recover in 2024. This recovery ended speculation that the DA might one day govern South Africa and curtailed the political prospects of the new workers' movement.

Economic development elsewhere in Africa played a major role in South Africa's recovery, as did a gradual improvement in the global economic outlook. Demand for services – from information technology to entertainment – ballooned on the continent on the back of huge investment flows into the resources, manufacturing, and retail industries. South Africa's entrepreneurs began to capitalise on providing services to Africa's booming economy.

South Africa surprised its critics to an extent that they hardly could have foreseen ten years ago. Its democracy has been consolidated largely as a result of a remarkable set of economic policy reforms, which in just one decade have transformed the lives of all South Africans.

More about the present

Today, in 2024, South Africa represents the best aspects of an emerging market. We are both a buoyant economy and a free and open society. As we compare ourselves with the rest of the world, it is difficult to identify a more exciting country to live in, or one that offers greater opportunities to the youth.

Our suburbs are clean and well kept. Townships are seeing massive improvements in infrastructure. This is driven both by state-led investment in roads, electricity, and water infrastructure and by private households extending and improving their homes. Crime and security remain major concerns, and many people believe policing should be toughened up. However, crime levels are declining, driven both by more effective policing and by better economic circumstances.

Children are able to access good education in suburban government schools, while South Africa's private schools remain among the best in the world. Research suggests that township and rural schools are also improving. Standards have been maintained in South Africa's mainstream universities, and certain faculties are global leaders in their fields.

While the middle classes, who are now predominantly black, continue to make use of private health care, even the government's harshest critics concede that standards at public hospitals and clinics have improved significantly since 1994. This reflects the overall improvements in public services inspired by the government's new-found commitment to merit, excellence, and the combating of corruption.

The business and investment environment is the best it has ever been. Levels of entrepreneurship now rival those of other emerging markets. The value of the stock market has more than doubled since 2014. Many young people are starting their own businesses. Small business owners are now seen as the major driver of employment and economic growth. Importantly, the accumulation of wealth no longer attracts the criticism of decades past. Investors are not viewed as enemies of the poor, and employers as exploiters of labour. Rather, business people and investors are seen as role models and patriots willing to risk their capital and commit their hard work to ensure that South Africa succeeds.

Larger investors are complimentary about the business environment. It is seen as a competitive investment space driven by a government that takes business seriously and goes out of its way to meet the demands of investors. Road, rail, electricity, and port infrastructure is expanding at an exponential rate to meet growing demand. The property rights of investors are secure, the rule of law prevails, and red tape has been cut to a minimum.

The evidence of a growing middle class can be seen all around. Blacks now constitute the biggest group of property buyers. Retailers report that black consumption expenditure is far more important than white. Malls are packed with black and white teenagers over weekends. One implication of middle-class growth is that South Africans have found it easier to unite behind the successes or failures of their sporting teams, regardless of the race of the players. The Springbok rugby team remains predominantly white, while Bafana Bafana remains predominantly black. However, this is also starting to change more rapidly, with selections driven by merit instead of policy.

Most importantly, South Africa remains a free and open society. There is a vibrant political opposition, although some leading DA figures of ten years ago have found a new home in the reformist ANC. Indeed, many former DA leaders now occupy prominent leadership positions in that ANC and its government. With little to distinguish the DA from the ANC in policy terms, its role as an opposition party has to an extent been supplanted by the militant and critical left-wing workers' movement that split away from the ANC during its reform years. However, the ANC's proven track record has limited the political prospects of these young radicals.

The government understands that strong and independent democratic institutions can be effective development partners that can help it achieve its social and economic objectives. In fact, throughout the reform years the government has relied on elements of the media and civil society to argue the merits of reform.

Road map to this future

One of the most useful aspects of this book is that it provides road maps for each of the four scenarios, listing the main route markers along the way from today until 2024. Should you see 80% or more of the road signs for a particular scenario in the months and years to follow, you can accept that that scenario is about to materialise. Should only a few of the route markers appear, you need to look at the other three scenarios.

Tickbox for the Wide Road	✓
Shortly after the 2014 election, a reform movement emerges within the ANC that challenges the dominant policy consensus on redistribution both within the party and in the court of public opinion.	◯

This movement warns that without significant economic reforms the ANC will lose an election within a decade.

The reform movement isolates the trade unions, which gives it more space for making new economic policy.

A left-wing 'workers' movement' gathers steam to oppose the ANC.

The ANC stops threatening the media, civil society, and the judiciary.

People with criminal records, or facing criminal charges, are removed from leadership positions in the ANC and government.

Property rights are entrenched and safeguarded.

The economy grows at 5% of GDP a year or more.

Investment inflows rise to levels on a par with those in leading emerging markets.

Entrepreneurship levels increase dramatically.

The saving rate increases from 15% to 25% of GDP.

Your experience of dealing with civil servants improves markedly after 2014.

The tax base expands significantly.

The unemployment rate starts to drop and is on its way to reaching 15% by 2024 from its current 25%.

The number of children passing mathematics in school with 50% or more is set to double by 2024.

A new wave of skilled technical graduates in fields ranging from IT to welding is entering the labour market.

Protest levels are declining, but not as a result of police action.

The inflation rate remains within the 3% to 6% target zone.

Soon after 2014, steps are taken to deregulate the labour market.

BEE and employment equity policies are diluted, and some provisions are abandoned.

Foreign investor protection agreements are renewed.

There is no further talk of nationalisation or the seizure of private assets, including farmland.

State corporations such as Eskom and SAA are auctioned off.

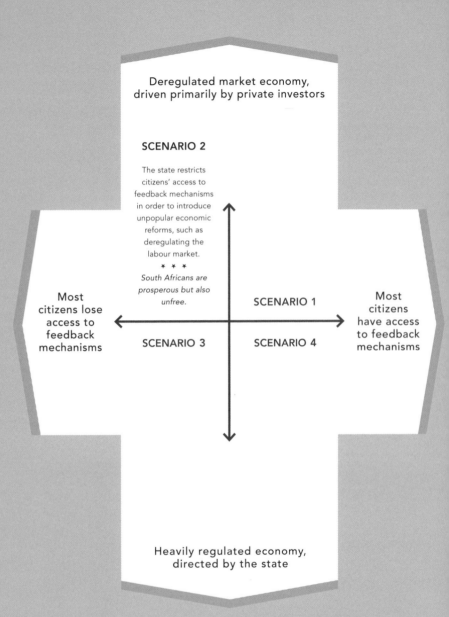

Deregulated market economy,
driven primarily by private investors

SCENARIO 2

The state restricts
citizens' access to
feedback mechanisms
in order to introduce
unpopular economic
reforms, such as
deregulating the
labour market.

* * *

*South Africans are
prosperous but also
unfree.*

SCENARIO 1

Most
citizens lose
access to
feedback
mechanisms

Most
citizens
have access
to feedback
mechanisms

SCENARIO 3

SCENARIO 4

Heavily regulated economy,
directed by the state

In the Narrow Road scenario the trend highways
lead us to a future where citizens are more prosperous
but have little freedom.

NARROW ROAD

(SCENARIO 2)[1]

It is May 2024. The ANC has won another election. The economy has been deregulated, and is growing rapidly, but the government has suppressed dissent and curtailed civil liberties in order to push through unpopular economic reforms. South Africa has exchanged liberty for prosperity, a trade-off that many citizens appear to have accepted.

South Africa remains a formal multiparty democracy, but the ANC has closed down democratic space by imposing restrictions on opposition parties as well as civil society and the media. This has allowed it to press ahead with initially unpopular economic reforms aimed at creating a less regulated market economy, including abolishing minimum wages, curbing the powers of trade unions, abandoning BEE and employment equity, and dumping environmental legislation. This has attracted new investment, and almost doubled the rate of economic growth.

Living standards are rising rapidly, based more on employment than welfare. Levels of education are improving. Life expectancy is on the rise, and the size of the middle class has doubled. Violent protests have abated, due to harsh police action as well as improved economic prospects.

South Africa now has a more closed political system and fewer civil liberties, combined with a growing market economy. The economic success of this model has secured its stability.

How did we get here?

Although the ANC won the 2014 election, service delivery protests continued unabated and opinion polls showed that confidence in the government had slipped to its lowest levels since 1994. These opinion poll results, together with the protest indicators, strengthened fears among party leaders that the party was entering a period of terminal decline.

Moreover, the party's declining popularity was matched by unprecedented internal and external conflict, as well as rising levels of criticism. For years, the ANC's alliance partners had acted as if they were opposition parties. COSATU leaders were especially consistent in publicly criticising the ANC and its leaders – often in the harshest terms. When, for example, the ANC government published its National Development Plan, the most scathing criticism came from its own alliance partners who threatened to disown the ANC if it did not abandon the plan. Likewise, when, in 2014, the ANC government launched a youth wage subsidy, in a desperate attempt to reduce the youth unemployment rate of more than 50%, its alliance partners threatened to scupper the plan.

The ANC also faced mounting criticism from other quarters. The media routinely ran exposés of corruption and government incompetence, even ridiculing the government. Many former ANC supporters in the media openly wrote of abandoning the party. This was an extraordinary change from the situation in 1994 when the media overwhelmingly welcomed the new ANC into government.

By 2014, civil society had also begun to turn against the government. Civil society organisations routinely challenged new government policies in court on issues ranging from policing to education, and often won. At times it appeared as if the government could not make any policy decision without some or the other activist organisation taking it to court.

Most worryingly for the ANC, however, the criticisms were accompanied by a resurgent political opposition – on both the right and the left of the party. By the 2014 election, support for the DA had increased more than tenfold since 1994. The DA was positioning itself as a party able to govern South Africa, and was winning new support from the black middle classes. Similarly, the radical left had established a formal political presence in the form of the EFF, and openly campaigned for policy shifts ranging from the confiscation of property to the nationalisation of mines, which many in the ANC knew would ruin the economy. Despite their moderate showing in the 2014 elections, opinion polls showed that the EFF was attracting considerable support, and the ANC understood that the radicals perhaps posed an even greater political threat than the DA.

Following the 2014 election, therefore, the ANC was under

siege. The roots of its problems were self-evident. By 2014, half of all young people were unemployed. Economic growth had slowed to just 2% despite the fact that growth of 5% was needed in order to make inroads into unemployment. Only half of children admitted to school were making it to matric, and only a third were passing. Only four out of every hundred learners were passing maths in matric. Growing investor uncertainty was curbing levels of investment. The budget deficit had grown to more than 5% of GDP. A small proportion of adults paid income tax, and people on social welfare outnumbered people with jobs.

The ANC also understood that its policies were not meeting popular expectations. BEE was a pillar of its policy framework, but catered for a small elite, and offered nothing to the poor and the unemployed. Employment equity also did nothing for the growing army of unemployed. Social welfare was not only effectively reducing poverty, but also raising expectations. Land reform was ineffective, and – with agriculture contributing only 3% of GDP – could never drive effective rural development. However, when the ANC tried to introduce new policy initiatives – such as the National Development Plan – its own alliance partners sabotaged its efforts, thereby hastening its political demise.

The growing onslaught against the party turned into a watershed for ANC leaders, who realised that without dramatic reforms the economy would not grow rapidly enough to save the party. However, these reforms would also not succeed as long as trade unions, civil society organisations, journalists, and radical political groupings were free to challenge them in the courts, the media, and on the streets. These challenges would delay implementation, and hasten the demise of the party.

Dubbed the 'new reformers', ANC leaders who subscribed to these views set in motion a ruthless campaign to save their party. The first objective was to suppress dissent about unpopular economic reforms. The party used its remaining political power, cadre deployment policies, the loyalty of its parliamentary caucus, and the power of patronage to change the rules of the political game.

The work of civil society organisations was curbed by limiting their fundraising abilities and monitoring their activities. For example, regulations were passed that prohibited the use of foreign funds for advocacy and lobbying work, while local donors were encouraged not to support 'oppositionist' civil society groups. In addition all civil society organisations had to re-register with the state and those that did not conform to regulations were closed down. The funding and activities of opposition parties were restricted. Laws were passed that restricted the ability of non-state actors to refer government policy and legislation to the courts.

The Judicial Service Commission was used to ensure growing judicial loyalty to the government. Errant judges were sanctioned, and independently minded judicial applicants were rejected. Cadre deployment was used to ensure that public servants remained loyal to the government and its policies. New laws were passed that curbed access to state information. Journalists were required to register, and were prohibited from publishing against the 'public interest'.

Local government, the health sector, the power sector, and the education sector were declared essential services, and strikes in those sectors were prohibited. Among other things, this meant that teachers and nurses could no longer go on strike. This weakened the core of the trade union movement. Recalcitrant union leaders were suspended, and their unions isolated in alliance politics. Laws restricting public protests were strictly enforced, and local authorities were encouraged to deny applications for marches and public protests.

South Africans soon found that the democratic space they had become accustomed to since 1994 had been curtailed to a significant extent. Any dissent met with the full force of the state. Journalists who broke the new media or security laws were arrested and detained. Civil society organisations that challenged the state lost their accreditation. Civil service managers who did not back party policy were replaced. Street protests were forcibly dispersed, and the protest leaders detained. ANC, SACP, and COSATU leaders who spoke out against the party line were brought up on internal disciplinary charges – and often criminal charges, especially for corruption. The business community was cowed into compliance.

This freed the ANC to act with impunity and introduce tough new economic reforms. These were very conservative and – ironically – drew comparisons to the reforms introduced in Britain by the late Margaret Thatcher. BEE and employment equity laws were largely abolished. The Labour Relations Act and Basic Conditions of Employment Act suffered a similar fate. Minimum wage laws were scrapped. Protectionist trade and investment policies were abandoned. Underperforming public enterprises were privatised. Environmental regulations such as carbon taxes on investors were abandoned. Land reform targets were abandoned, and white farmers were encouraged to invest in their businesses in order to safeguard future food security. Red tape for investors was slashed across the board.

The results were as impressive as in Thatcherite Britain. Investment levels increased dramatically to match, and later exceed, emerging market norms. Economic growth spurted first to 5% and then to more than 6%. Unemployment fell from more than 25% to 15%. Given the more flexible labour market, productivity improved, thus boosting South Africa's global competitiveness. Exports rose, and the current account deficit fell from more than 5% in 2014 to 3%. Given higher employment levels and higher earnings, tax revenues rose quickly, enabling the government to reduce the budget deficit, improve services, and increase state spending on vital infrastructure. The savings rate rose to 25% of GDP.

The drive for efficiency and investment saw the emergence of a much more professional civil service – even as loyalty to the state was enforced. One consequence was that the quality of health care in government hospitals improved significantly, as once-recalcitrant nurses started to change their attitude. A growing tax base also meant that more money was invested in the public health system.

This also happened in education. The government realised that school-leavers needed to be more literate and numerate to take advantage of the opportunities on offer in the newly buoyant economy. Teachers or school principles had to perform or get out. Numeracy and literacy improved markedly, and the calibre of school-leavers improved. Given increased state resources, more of these school-leavers were offered free access to higher education. The number of skilled professionals increased, further bolstering the economy and attracting new investment.

Law and order were now more strictly enforced. Dissent was ruthlessly suppressed, and often-brutal police action resulted in significant drops in violent crime. This won the support of the law-abiding public, much to the dismay of local and international human rights activists.

Throughout the reform process the government had under-stood that South Africa's long-term stability would ultimately depend on the economic impact of the reform programme on households throughout the country. If people's lives did not improve, resentment about the crackdown on freedom and civil liberties could easily escalate into a national uprising on a scale that would overwhelm the new security laws. The government therefore urgently needed to improve the economic prospects of ordinary people. Fortunately, this began to happen early on in the reform process.

Given higher growth and employment levels, poverty and inequality dropped sharply in the years after 2014. At the same time, rising tax revenues enabled the government to main-tain, and even expand, its welfare programme. However, state welfare was no longer the sole driver of improved living stand-ards. This was a vital change as it meant that South Africans were seeing their living standards improve through their own efforts. This new sense of self-worth cemented their loyalty to the ANC and support for its economic reforms.

For the first time since 1994, the incomes of black households rose more rapidly than those of white households. This did not mean that whites were becoming poorer, but that income gaps were starting to close. For example, by 2019 more blacks than whites were holding senior management positions, serving as company directors, buying property in urban and rural areas, accessing private medical aid, and enrolling their children in private schools.

The white middle class also benefited from the new dispensation. Rather than seeking to curtail the participation of whites in the economy, the ANC government encouraged and utilised white skills, capital, and entrepreneurship to catalyse economic growth. This, in turn, created enhanced opportunities for the new black middle class, which was key to ensuring the success of the reform efforts.

In this way, the reform movement ensured that all South Africans benefited from the reforms of the past decade. Young black people found work, the black middle class grew quickly, and the future of the white middle class was secured. The business community benefited from a favourable investment environment. In a future that could never have been predicted, the government had succeeded in persuading citizens to accept restrictions on their liberty, in exchange for meeting their socio-economic expectations.

More about the present

South Africa today is a very different society from that in 2014. In the era immediately after 1994, South Africans enjoyed high levels of freedom, but suffered from poor governance and an underperforming economy. Today, they are far less free, but have a far more effective government and a booming economy. As a result, they have come to embrace the reform movement, even though it has removed some of their freedoms.

Suburbs are clean and well kept. Municipal services are of a high standard. There are no more billing crises. Traffic lights work, and every intersection has street signs. Visitors to municipal offices are treated with respect, and municipal staff are proud of their jobs and their municipalities.

Levels of serious and violent crime have dropped significantly. South Africa is still a violent country, and there are allegations of poor prison conditions and the torture and even the extra-judicial execution of suspected criminals by the police. However, South Africans have shown that they are willing to live with these abuses of power and diminished rights in exchange for higher levels of personal safety.

Government schools are improving, and more middle-class parents are sending their children to these schools, even though they can afford private education. Private schools remain elitist institutions producing skilled and well-educated young people who can compete with the best in the world. The universities are internationally competitive, and tuition is virtually free for all matriculants who qualify for further study. Many new study opportunities have also been created in technical colleges.

Visiting a public hospital, police station, or government

department is no longer the distressing experience it was ten years ago. Public servants have become exactly that – servants of the public. They are far more accountable, and many people comment on how far civil servants are going to help them resolve queries or obtain the documents they require.

Urban centres are hives of activity as new shopping malls and other retail developments are constructed. Inside these new facilities, an increasingly integrated middle class is driving a consumer boom that has bolstered South Africa's economic recovery. The social divide is now more about class than about race. Apart from being more racially integrated, life in the suburbs has not changed much from the 1970s and 1980s.

Development is not restricted to former white suburbs. Former black townships and even informal settlements are also experiencing a boom in retail activity and housing construction. Forecasts now suggest that over the next two generations the bulk of South Africans are set to move into the middle classes.

This trend is reflected in higher levels of business and investor confidence. The fear of South Africa giving up its place as the leading economy on the continent to Nigeria, Egypt, or Morocco has receded. Other African economies are also performing well, but South Africa remains leagues ahead in terms of skills, infrastructure, and per capita income levels. South Africa is Africa's investment leader, and one of the world's most prominent emerging markets.

There are rumours of corruption at the highest levels of state. At dinner parties, hilarious – if hair-raising – stories are told about which party leader or government official had to be bought off to secure permission to build a mall or obtain a mining contract. But these issues are not aired in public, as this would attract the unwelcome attention of the state and the ruling party.

The ANC now rules with impunity, and countenances little resistance or dissent. Very few people are prepared to challenge or criticise the state. Newscasts are bland, and focus on undisputed economic successes. There is no reporting on official corruption or malfeasance.

The political opposition is cowed at times and ineffective at others – this is as true of the left-wing radical opposition as of the DA. In the current climate, the opposition attracts far less support than ten years ago, in part because such support is frowned upon by the ruling party, but also because so many South Africans are grateful for the economic progress and security offered by the refocused ANC. Middle-class whites and blacks are often heard to remark that this is exactly how the country needs to be governed – with a fair but firm hand.

Some courageous journalists and activists continue to criticise the government and advocate for greater freedom of speech and the restoration of civil liberties. When they become too vocal for the government's liking, they are detained under various security laws. Some have gone into exile, to continue their campaigns from abroad. There are rumours of harsh conditions in detention centres, but these allegations never make it to court or appear in the media.

This model of authoritarian control combined with economic progress is also taking hold elsewhere in Africa. South Africa is often compared to China. Looking towards the future, the key question – as in the case of China – is whether this model is sustainable, or whether growing economic prosperity will again drive increased demands for greater individual liberty.

Road map to this future

If we are headed for this future, you should be able to identify 80% or more of the road signs set out below. If you do not, you need to turn to the route maps of the other three scenarios.

Tickbox for the Narrow Road	✓
A new reformist group rises to prominence in the ANC.	◯
Following the 2014 elections, the ANC and the government develop a firm new consensus that prioritises economic growth over redistribution.	◯
Trade unions are marginalised, and dissenting COSATU and SACP leaders are excluded from key government positions.	◯
The reformist group moves to end dissent and infighting in the ANC and tripartite alliance.	◯
The government introduces new measures for regulating the media and civil society.	◯

Controls over access to state information are tightened.

The Judicial Service Commission appoints judges sympathetic to the ruling party.

Regulations for the registration, fundraising and campaigning of political parties are tightened.

The government tampers with the voters' roll.

State institutions including the police, the revenue services, and intelligence agencies are used to settle political scores within the ANC and harass opposition leaders, civil society, and the media.

The rate of economic growth rises to more than 5% of GDP.

Investment levels reach 25% of GDP.

Unemployment begins to recede and seems set to reach 15% in 2024.

The number of children passing maths in matric rises rapidly.

The current account deficit and budget deficit improve.

The number of taxpayers increases significantly.

Inflation remains in its target zone.

Social welfare grants increase in value, exceeding the rate of inflation.

The proportion of people with formal jobs as opposed to people receiving welfare increases significantly.

Labour regulations are watered down and in some cases scrapped.

BEE and employment equity policies are also watered down or scrapped.

Investment protection agreements are respected.

Property rights are guaranteed.

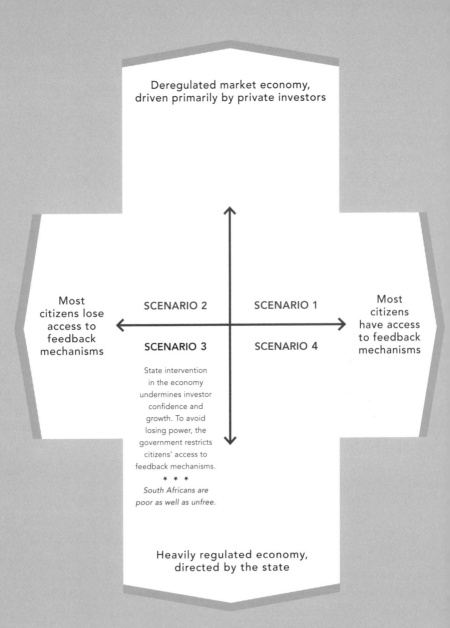

Deregulated market economy,
driven primarily by private investors

Most
citizens lose
access to
feedback
mechanisms

SCENARIO 2

SCENARIO 1

Most
citizens
have access
to feedback
mechanisms

SCENARIO 3

SCENARIO 4

State intervention
in the economy
undermines investor
confidence and
growth. To avoid
losing power, the
government restricts
citizens' access to
feedback mechanisms.

* * *

*South Africans are
poor as well as unfree.*

Heavily regulated economy,
directed by the state

In the Rocky Road scenario the trend highways
lead us into a future where citizens are much poorer
and have little freedom.

ROCKY ROAD

(SCENARIO 3)[1]

It is May 2024. A corrupt and radical black-nationalist regime has just won a violent and disputed election, and rules South Africa with an iron grip. Civil liberties have been eroded. Damaged by misguided state intervention, the economy is in recession, and living standards have suffered a precipitous decline. Industries have been nationalised, and private property confiscated. Those who can are leaving the country. The world weeps for South Africa, but most South Africans are powerless to escape from their plight.

Riled by electoral setbacks, the ANC has fallen in with the radical left and wrecked democratic institutions as part of a drive to rule by decree. Constitutional principles have been eroded or ignored. Judges have been bent to the will of the state. Newspapers have been closed down, and prominent journalists jailed. Human rights activists have been harassed and terrorised by agents of the state. The opposition is fighting a futile rearguard action to reinstate a proper democracy.

In line with political oppression, the economy has suffered irreparable harm as policy-makers sought to implement reckless populist ideas. Property rights have been eroded, and much private land, as well as many businesses, has been expropriated. Price controls have triggered rampant inflation, and the rand has lost much of its value. The economy has been in recession for several years.

The economic decline has triggered a social crisis. Living standards have fallen for the first time since 1994. Unemployment has worsened almost every year during the past decade. Inflation has undermined the value of social welfare. Food production has fallen significantly on the back of the expropriation of commercial farms. Hospitals are starved for funds and lack basic equipment and medication. Schools are in a state of disrepair, and most government services are worsening.

South Africa now represents the archetypal African worst-case scenario of a ruthless and incompetent nationalist regime undermining democracy to cement its grip on power, and dictating to a cowed population, destroying the economy in the process. There seems to be no hope of recovery, and South Africans are shocked by the speed with which this political and economic catastrophe has overtaken them.

How did we get here?

While the ANC won the 2014 election, many of its former supporters stayed away from the polls, and the opposition vote grew further. This was true for the DA as well as for new parties on the political left that had split from the ANC and the trade union movement. In fact, the EFF gave a surprisingly strong showing in the election and gained a number of parliamentary seats. Together with rising levels of anti-government protest, ANC leaders therefore realised they were in a lot of political and economic trouble.

The source of this trouble was easy to diagnose. Economic growth was too slow to draw the majority of black people into the formal economy, and the party was therefore unable to meet popular expectations. Where living standards had increased, this was driven by state welfare rather than employment. In fact, by 2014 welfare payments were reaching more than 15 million people, while only 12 million people had jobs, and only 6 million paid income tax. This was not a sustainable way of meeting the expectations of poor South Africans. For example, despite living standards increasing due to social grants and free services, data also showed that, despite 20 years of democracy, the household income gap between black and white households had broadened. Moreover, South Africa's Gini coefficient – a composite indicator of social inequality – had worsened. Most damningly, by 2014 more than 50% of young people were unemployed.

As unemployment and inequality increased, so did the impatience of South Africa's young people, which spurred a new brand of economic and political radicalism. This featured calls for the nationalisation of mining and other industrial sectors, and the confiscation of land without compensation. These calls were accompanied by a virulent racial nationalism that saw whites described as 'criminals', and black migrants from elsewhere in Africa subjected to what amounted to pogroms. These calls did not just emanate from within poor communities but reflected a growing racial nationalism within more prosperous black communities as well, and were increasingly echoed by prominent black commentators in the media. Initially, most analysts and observers, as well as the business community, wrote off these radical and nationalist calls as the fantasies of marginal groupings that could not possibly have a broader impact. As a result, they were not taken seriously, which proved to be a major miscalculation.

The ANC was not as naive. It remembered the contribution of disenchanted young people to the struggle against the apartheid state; after all, it was schoolchildren who moved the anti-apartheid struggle into high gear during the Soweto uprising of 1976. The ANC also knew that, in the 2014 election, the number of young voters who stayed away from the polls had matched those who voted for the ANC. It further understood that its former supporters were turning to violent service delivery protests and opposition parties. At the time of the 2014 elections, the police were dealing with several anti-government protests a day. The ANC therefore recognised the danger presented by the formation of the EFF, which advocated precisely the brand of radical politics and economics that was gaining ground among many former ANC supporters.

The ANC's political position was further weakened by the fact that the DA had adopted many of its principles and policies, and even appropriated its political icons. The DA embraced BEE, and supported legislation containing new penalties for employers who failed to implement racial equity goals. It also advocated accelerating and expanding the transfer of commercial agricultural land to black farmers under the Land Reform Programme. However, while increasingly invading the ANC's policy space, it continued to condemn corruption and incompetence in the ANC government. This 'new and better ANC' (or 'ANC-lite' as the DA was called) began to attract some of the ANC's best members and supporters, particularly moderate young professionals. The DA's adoption of numerous ANC policies, together with its model of clean and effective government, also saw it attract greater support from the media and influential civil society organisations, and its media profile improved dramatically. The DA was becoming the ANC of 1994 as the ANC's popularity took a nosedive.

Despite these clear signs of the ANC's decline, political intransigence, ideological stubbornness, and growing internal racial nationalism resulted in its leaders resisting calls for reform. Moderate and reformist members were pilloried. Offended by this behaviour, and distressed at ongoing government corruption and incompetence, many leading figures left the government and the party.

As the ANC shed its best people, it also lost the capacity to reform. As a result, despite mounting crises of investment, unemployment, and governance, nothing was done to create a more enabling space for investors, improve economic competitiveness, or tackle growing corruption. Nothing was done to improve the quality of education, or reform labour laws or empowerment regulations. Rather, the party (and government) increasingly came to echo the rallying cry of the radical left that the private sector and 'the whites' had failed to redistribute the country's wealth, and that the state should now do so. The party turned to radical political and economic rhetoric in an attempt to discredit the now predominantly black DA and, in so doing, threw in its lot with the EFF and the black-nationalist radicals.

The government's calls for the state-led redistribution of national wealth initially won much support from the left-leaning media, some trade unions, and many civil society organisations that were hostile to private capital and favoured a powerful redistributionist state. The idea grew that the business community had failed to stick to its promises to redistribute wealth on a voluntary basis, and that the state should now intervene. While the ANC had long engaged in such rhetoric, it had seldom acted on it. However, after 2014 the new ANC leadership started to turn this rhetoric into policy and used its still-significant parliamentary majority, together with cadre deployment and the power of patronage, to enforce a number of policy shifts.

First, the state placed itself at the centre of the economy, as both player and referee. State-owned enterprises in agriculture, banking, mining, and construction were established to compete with the private sector. The government also passed draconian expropriation legislation, which led in later years to many private businesses being nationalised in what were effectively free-carry public-private partnerships. To make these industries competitive, price controls and export curbs were introduced in respect of 'strategic goods' ranging from coal to scrap iron. Thousands of hectares of commercial farmland were nationalised, and fell into disuse.

In the economic turmoil that followed, the government hastily adopted a series of laws further tightening up labour market controls as well as BEE and employment equity in a bid to curb job losses and disinvestment. The results were catastrophic. Hundreds of thousands of jobs were lost as the government tightened its control over the economy. The prices of basic goods and services increased very quickly on the back of falling production, higher input costs, and a weakening rand. For example, given the currency slide, the price of fuel doubled within a few months.

An alarmed government moved quickly to place curbs on retrenchments and price controls on food and basic goods, but this merely fuelled hoarding and shortages. Supermarket shelves, even in middle-class neighbourhoods, began to empty. Equally desperate efforts to hike tariff barriers, in order to protect local consumers against price increases, merely contributed to spiralling inflation and shortages of consumer goods. Inflation, which had moved well beyond its target zone after 2014, began to climb exponentially.

As the crisis deepened ahead of the 2019 election, an increasingly paranoid and defensive government began to use even more hostile rhetoric against the business sector, Western countries, and white South Africans. In fits of racial nationalism, it blamed these groups collectively and individually for sabotaging the economy. Measures for enforcing BEE and employment equity were stepped up as the ANC government tried to force the contracting business and investment community to 'increase its contribution to the South African economy'. It threatened to jail company directors who failed to 'promote economic growth', and seize companies that failed to act 'in the national interest'.

These draconian measures were aimed not only at regaining the support of increasingly disaffected citizens, but also at allowing party officials to seize and strip company assets in an orgy of self-enrichment similar to the Zimbabwean 'indigenisation' and land reform policies a decade earlier. South African companies began receiving government notices instructing them to surrender portions of their operations to the state, or face expropriation and expulsion from the country.

The 2019 election results were a predictable setback for the ruling party that saw its support levels drop by several percentage points as the economic consequences of its radical economic policies were felt in households around the country. The DA gained more than a third of the vote in that election and looked set to win in 2024. In the aftermath of the election, public protest levels took off and reached record highs.

The state took swift action against those it blamed for 'sabotaging the economy'. As growth tumbled and inflation rose, ever more interventionist economic policies were proposed. More land was seized for redistribution on the grounds that white farmers were causing food shortages and price increases. Likewise, more productive industries received notices instructing them to surrender portions of their shareholdings and enter into partnerships with the state.

Calamity turned into farce as the government wiped out all the progress made during the first 20 years of democracy. As the world looked on in awe, and South Africans in horror, the country saw its economy go into a tailspin. Investment flows were non-existent. The rand had lost more than half of its value, and was still tumbling. Inflation was climbing exponentially. Tax receipts had plummeted, and debt and deficit levels effectively curtailed the ability of the government to implement any of its policies.

Living standards dropped for the first time since 1994 as inflation and rising unemployment destroyed the value of social grants. Due to budget constraints, the quality of free and subsidised state services declined. Larger town and urban areas were without water for days on end, and power outages were a regular occurrence. Cadre deployment spread further as an increasingly corrupt party made room for its supporters and their family and friends in the civil service – many of these exiles from the collapsing private sector. Anyone who needed a document such as a passport or driver's licence had to know someone in the relevant department, and pay a bribe to get it. Infrastructure from roads to street lights fell into decay.

Middle-class households and the political opposition became increasingly vocal as the value of their investments fell and the state seized more of their property. Those who could emigrate did so, but the bulk of the population had no way out.

Protest levels had continued to build after the 2019 election and a national uprising seemed possible as the political opposition, think-tanks, civil society, the media, and the protest movement came together to demand change. This was despite the fact that many activists, especially in civil society, had initially endorsed the ANC's leftward economic policy shifts, while a number of media commentators had endorsed the racial nationalism that lay at the centre of South Africa's economic demise.

While the government was shocked by the failure of its economic reforms, it refused to change its course. Rather, it turned to propaganda to protect itself, and anti-white and anti-business rhetoric reached new highs. Party leaders and government representatives routinely attacked these group-ings, blaming them for the state of the country. However, this time the rhetoric did not work – and the protests esca-lated further, while opinion polls showed a calamitous drop in support for the ruling party. South Africans were seeing their living standards decline and the public increasingly turned their anger on the government.

Ruling party leaders, who were becoming accustomed to acting with impunity, now believed there was only one way to secure their political survival, namely to tear down democratic institutions and stamp out dissent. Using its still-considerable political majority, and the loyalty bought with cadre deploy-ment policies, the party swiftly set about dismantling South Africa's democratic institutions. Laws were passed restricting access to information, as well as the scope of reporting in the media. Journalists and editors who violated these laws were eligible for arrest and imprisonment. The activities and fund-raising efforts of civil society organisations were restricted. Those that routinely criticised the government saw their reve-nues collapse, or were deregistered by executive fiat. White critics were hounded as racists and colonists who should leave the country. Black critics were described as sell-outs who were threatening the revolution and acting in cahoots with whites.

Police acted ruthlessly to stamp out street protests, and protest leaders were arrested. The Judicial Service Commission was used to bring to heel judges deemed to be acting 'against the national interest'. New appointees to the bench were staunch supporters of the state. Business leaders who spoke out were threatened with asset seizures, and the withdrawal of government contracts. The intelligence agencies were used to spy on, detain, interrogate, and intimidate people suspected of acting against the state.

Journalists could no longer freely report on corruption and maladministration, and those who did suffered unpleasant visits from the police and intelligence agencies. Civil society organisations became ineffective, as their finances dried up. Alarmingly for both groups, appeals to the courts for protection against arbitrary state action began to fail. Brutal riot-policing methods and the intimidation and arrest of protest leaders saw a marked decline in levels of public protest. Members of poor communities suffering from service break-downs were now too intimidated to challenge the state. The DA suffered from intimidation, electoral fraud, and funding shortages. At the same time, they no longer had a media plat-form for political campaigning.

In what would have seemed almost unthinkable a decade previously, South Africa became a facade democracy with an authoritarian ruling party presiding over a mismanaged and declining economy. Worse still, citizens had only limited means of resistance as the media were cowed, civil society had no resources, the independence of the judiciary had been undermined, and the private sector bent to the will of the state.

More about the present

In both political and economic terms, South Africa has slipped a long way over the past 30 years. Once lauded as the 'rainbow nation', and a world-leading example of a successful democratic transition, it has turned into a banana republic. Its economy, which showed so much promise in the early years after 1994, has succumbed to the same devastating brand of Afro-socialism that wrecked so many post-colonial societies on the continent, including Zimbabwe.

One only needs to drive through the middle-class suburbs to see the extent of the damage. Road markings have faded, many street lights are out, and roads are potholed. Crime is rampant, with the police being the perpetrators as well as the guardians. What remains of the middle classes live in enclaves behind high walls and electric fences, patrolled by vicious dogs and armed guards. Power outages are routine, and most middle-class households have back-up generators.

Shops in wealthier neighbourhoods are generally well stocked, but prices are prohibitive and basics ranging from petrol to eggs are sometimes in short supply. Poorer areas have become slums in which households subsist on what is left of the state's social welfare programme, ravaged by inflation. Gaining access to basics such as clean water has become part of their daily routine. Child malnutrition rates are climbing, and waterborne diseases are driving increases in child mortality rates.

Public education has largely collapsed, and schools are routinely without books or learning materials. Hospitals lack basic equipment and medicines. The private health care sector has shrunk but remains resilient, and now caters to the political elite and what remains of the upper middle classes. Government offices are dirty and offer poor services, and bribes are necessary to secure identify documents, birth certificates, and driver's licences.

Standards at South Africa's universities have fallen, and wealthier people now ensure that their children attend private schools and qualify to enter universities overseas. Their classmates at these elite schools include the children of party leaders. Tens of thousands of young South Africans, black and white, are leaving the country for opportunities in Europe, Australia, the Middle East, and North America. Even resurgent African economies, which now grow more rapidly and attract more investment than South Africa, are drawing skilled professional people away.

Many businesses have withdrawn, in successive waves of disinvestment. Key industries such as mining and agriculture are being resuscitated by Chinese investors, and Chinese workers are a common sight in rural and mining areas. However, the economy weakens further, and up to 70% of young people are unemployed.

Newspapers are bland and full of pro-government propaganda. The little business and investment activity that exists is facilitated with bribes paid to party leaders and government officials. Courageous human rights activists live a dangerous life; many have been jailed, while others continue their activism from abroad.

South Africans face a bleak future. They are angry that they were so easily persuaded to surrender the political and economic freedoms they had won in 1994, but they are unlikely to win them back in the foreseeable future.

Road map to this future

If we are headed for this future, you should be able to identify 80% or more of the road signs set out below. If you do not, you need to look at the route maps to the other three scenarios.

Tickbox for the Rocky Road	✓
The ANC refuses to reform the economy, which remains in the doldrums, eventually moving into recession.	○
The ANC isolates reformist leaders and even expels them from the party.	○
The ANC echoes the radical policy perspectives of the EFF and similar extremist groups, and later rallies behind these young radicals.	○
The SACP and some COSATU leaders gain a greater foothold in the ANC, and begin to dominate its policy-making mechanisms.	○
The ANC develops a nasty brand of racial nationalism and routinely describes its critics as enemies of the state and counter-revolutionaries.	○
Key black commentators and opinion formers begin to endorse the new regime's racial nationalism.	○

Some journalists and civil society role players begin to suggest that the state could do a better job of redistributing wealth than the private sector.

The government proposes measures for curbing the freedom of the media and civil society, and the independence of the judiciary.

The state proposes laws that will allow it to seize private property.

The police and the security services begin to monitor the activities of government critics.

The state begins to use 'dirty tricks' to undermine opposition parties, and manipulate the outcomes of elections.

The budget deficit remains significantly higher than the rate of economic growth.

The trade deficit far outstrips those of comparable emerging markets.

Ratings agencies downgrade South Africa as an investment destination.

The rand weakens further against the US dollar.

Certain high-profile companies withdraw from South Africa.

Inflation far exceeds its target band. ○

Tax receipts decline. ○

The proportion of people on welfare compared with people working continues to increase. ○

Poverty levels and child and maternal mortality rates are increasing. ○

Water and electricity services are regularly disrupted. ○

The government blames investors, business people, and entrepreneurs for the problems confronting the country, and many members of the public begin to support this view. ○

Property rights are eroded, and the first farms are expropriated. ○

Stricter BEE and employment equity policies as well as labour regulations are proposed. ○

A number of new state-owned businesses emerge and try to compete with the private sector. ○

Organised business does little to defend private enterprise. ○

The state proposes a range of tax increases, price controls, and protectionist measures in a last-ditch effort to save the economy from implosion.

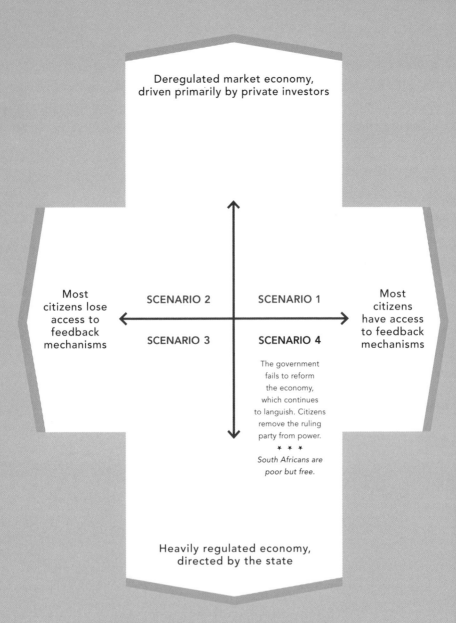

Deregulated market economy,
driven primarily by private investors

Most
citizens lose
access to
feedback
mechanisms

SCENARIO 2 | SCENARIO 1

SCENARIO 3 | SCENARIO 4

Most
citizens
have access
to feedback
mechanisms

The government
fails to reform
the economy,
which continues
to languish. Citizens
remove the ruling
party from power.

✳ ✳ ✳

South Africans are
poor but free.

Heavily regulated economy,
directed by the state

In the Toll Road scenario the trend
highways lead us into a future where many citizens
are poor, but free.

TOLL ROAD

(SCENARIO 4)[1]

It is May 2024. After sliding for a decade, the ANC has just lost the recent election, and a DA president now occupies the Union Buildings – albeit by the narrowest of electoral margins. The economy is weak, and levels of unemployment remain very high. Living standards have fallen.

Another decade of infighting, corruption, incompetence, and policy confusion saw the ANC lose the 2024 election to a coalition led by the DA. This outcome was inevitable, as opinion polls showed that more and more South Africans were losing faith in the ANC. Assisted by a free and powerful media and civil society organisations, the DA led a coalition that skilfully exploited the ANC's declining popularity.

The ANC owes much of its demise to trends in the economic sphere in the decade leading up to 2024. Economic growth languished below 3% of GDP, and levels of unemployment remained stubbornly high. Income levels barely kept pace with inflation, and state welfare remained a dominant source of income for half of all households. Despite this, the ANC stubbornly refused to accept that its economic policies were outdated and ineffective, and in need of some drastic reforms.

Due to poor economic performance, the socio-economic circumstances of South Africans stagnated. Nothing was done to improve the quality of education. No rural development took place. Public health care services remained poor.

South Africa now faces a new and daunting future as the untested DA government sets about seeking to meet the expectations of South Africans for employment, good education, and the opportunity to improve their own lives. However, it is still unclear whether it has the capacity or the policies to rebuild the economy.

How did we get here?

The 2014 election result was not the massive setback for the ANC that many commentators were expecting, as its share of the vote remained above 60%. While DA support had grown, and the radical left had made a small showing, the ANC seemed to have kept these two political adversaries in check. This was despite the fact that growing service delivery protests and opinion poll results had caused some analysts to speculate that the party might suffer a dramatic reversal of fortune at the polls. Yet, the ANC managed to maintain a significant parliamentary majority despite the fact that half of young people were unemployed, levels of inequality remained high, and economic growth dwindled at around 2%, making South Africa one of the slowest growing economies in Africa.

In retrospect, its relatively good showing at the 2014 polls could probably be ascribed to two factors. The first was that 50% of people were directly or indirectly benefiting from state welfare – outnumbering those participating in the formal economy. Despite growing disaffection with the party, it was still seen as responsible for improving the living standards of most black people, which helped it to retain a measure of political loyalty. The second was that no alternative political force had yet emerged that could challenge the ANC's hegemony. The DA was still busy rebranding itself, and would only reap the dividends in later elections. The EFF and COPE were attracting small numbers of fringe voters and did not have the capacity to rival the ANC and the DA.

The ANC (and many South Africans) therefore entered the post-2014 election era with a degree of complacency, which proved to be misplaced. However, this was not true of everyone. The DA, for one, understood that the ANC was far more vulnerable than the 2014 election results suggested. Notably, while the ANC's share of the actual vote remained well above 60%, its share of the potential vote had fallen from more than 50% in 1994 to less than 40% in 2014. Absent voters outnumbered those who had voted for the ANC, and its apparent political dominance was therefore something of an illusion. Likewise, opinion poll data showed that people were supporting the ANC with increasing reluctance, and could switch to the DA if the ANC failed to meet their expectations *and* the DA transformed into a more appealing political option for dissatisfied ANC supporters.

In retrospect, it was clear that in 2014 voters had given the ANC one last chance to deliver on its promises before taking the significant step of abandoning the party they believed had liberated the country and had done much to improve their lives after 1994. Similarly, it became clear that the ANC was so blinded by arrogance or ideology that it simply could not comprehend this, or, if it did, that it simply did not have the unity and capacity to reform the economy rapidly enough to ward off its political demise.

The ANC government therefore made no attempt to introduce policy reforms aimed at ensuring higher levels of investment, economic growth, and job creation. Rather, it bumbled along with a contradictory set of policy ideas that continued to harm the economy. To many observers the government seemed paralysed when it came to improving growth levels and boosting job creation. Furthermore, at precisely the time when economic growth threatened to dip below 2% of GDP, the government proposed fines – some as high as 10% of turnover – on firms that violated BEE and employment equity regulations. Likewise, the DTI proposed jail terms for unregistered entrepreneurs – in a country with the lowest levels of entrepreneurship in all five BRICS countries. This was a bizarre step in an economy that desperately needed more investment and entrepreneurship, and a great example of the disconnect that developed between the policies of the ANC and the needs of the country and the economy.

The business community was equally complacent. It

dismissed ideas that economic policies were not working, or that the economy was in trouble. Critical think-tanks and commentators were dismissed as prophets of doom. South Africans were urged to 'work together' and ensure 'social harmony', which was ironic given that key government policies were working against this.

It was seen as politically incorrect to question whether BEE and employment equity, for example, were slowing economic growth – hence very few analysts, let along business leaders, said much in public about the negative impact of government policy on growth and investment.

Likewise, it was seen as provocative to ask whether South Africa's stringent labour laws were contributing to unemployment. Ten years previously, safeguarding the rights of workers was seen as paramount, and questioning those rights as politically incorrect and even conservative or reactionary. Therefore, when, in 2013, the government hiked minimum wages for farm workers by 50%, few senior business, political or civil society leaders protested. Those who did were described as 'racists' seeking 'to exploit workers' and 'retard agricultural transformation'. Within months, 30 000 jobs, affecting the livelihoods of 250 000 people, had been lost. Yet trade unions and business leaders described these job losses as 'mild' and 'lower than initially predicted'. There seemed to be no sense of urgency and crisis.

Political correctness also prevented many role players from stating the truth about the public schooling system. Studies showed that the quality of maths and science teaching in South African schools was among the worst in the world. In private, many employers complained that school leavers were barely literate. Yet the government continued to declare that the education system was progressing, and that criticism was both racist and alarmist.

The same was true for the state of the government and the civil service itself. By 2014, corruption seemed rampant, but very few transgressors were called to task, let alone sent to prison. The media reported on instances of corruption at all levels of government, from the national level through the provinces down to metro and small-town municipalities. While much was said about the seriousness of corruption, nothing appeared to be done about it.

A bizarre pantomime was playing itself out. Half of South Africans were unemployed, and townships and informal settlements were caught in a new cycle of violent protest. Reckless government policy was putting the brakes on investment. Yet people in power went about their business suggesting that things were not as bad as they seemed, and that the country would soon turn the corner. When asked why the economy was growing so slowly, government leaders used excuses ranging from the global economic slump to the legacy of apartheid. Yet other emerging markets – including other former colonies – were growing twice as rapidly. Politicians and business leaders seldom mentioned domestic economic policy as a major cause of the country's poor economic performance.

The ANC's intransigence was a heaven-sent opportunity for the DA. As the ANC's popularity declined on the back of incompetence and corruption, the DA was positioning itself as a clean and effective alternative. In a shrewd move, it also increasingly adopted ANC policies on issues ranging from land reform to BEE. As a result, the DA was able to offer voters a simple choice: they could choose a clean government over a corrupt government without having to abandon BEE, affirmative action and land reform. This was a political masterstroke by the DA's tacticians, even if it represented a move away from its liberal roots. Black voters suddenly found it easier to associate themselves with the DA, as it reflected ideals similar to those of the ANC.

It was a masterstroke for a second reason in that it undermined growing left-wing radical sentiment among young black people who now found new hope in the charismatic young DA leaders. In the process, the DA shed the last of its truly liberal office bearers – but this was a price it was prepared to pay. Between 2014 and 2019 the party also implemented a policy of aggressive affirmative action in its own ranks in order to present the electorate with a more representative face. It elected its first black leader, and by 2019 almost every provincial and national DA leader and spokesperson was black.

While the DA headed anti-ANC sentiment in the country, the media, civil society, and the radical left were not far behind. In the run-up to the 2019 election, many journalists (except for those working for the SABC) sharply criticised the ruling party, particularly due to corruption and incompetence. Exposés of party leaders looting the public purse became routine. Activist journalism became an important tool in the arsenal of forces that aimed to work the ANC out of power. Civil society organisations also stepped up the ante against the ANC, utilising the courts, Chapter 9 institutions, and public protests. This lobby was fuelled by evidence of corruption, incompetence and stagnating living standards and spiralling unemployment. Civil society leaders routinely accused the ANC of having failed to deliver on its promises to South Africa's people. Radical young political leaders accused the ANC of being in cahoots with 'business' and 'colonisers' and having abandoned the liberation struggle.

While the ANC often reacted angrily, lashing out at journalists and radical youth leaders alike, its bark proved worse than its bite. While it threatened sanctions against civil society, it seemed unable to act on these threats as infighting and incompetence in the party stymied effective responses. Despite being attacked from every quarter, the ANC seemed unwilling and unable to mount an effective response beyond stepped up rhetoric. Therefore, it came as no surprise when ANC support in the 2019 elections dropped to well under 60% of votes cast. Effectively, voters signalled that they were tired of giving the party yet another chance.

In the aftermath of that election, the last of the pragmatic ANC leaders tried to warn the party that it was in deep political trouble, and that a continued failure to address corruption and reform economic policy could result in it being toppled at the polls. They won some support in the business press and some conservative think-tanks, but very little within their own party. Voices of reform were isolated, and pilloried within the tripartite alliance. The reasons for this were twofold.

First, calls for action against corruption threatened the vested interests of too many party members. It was widely known that corruption extended to the top echelons in the party and government. Many party leaders and their side-kicks in government did a roaring trade in corrupt deals and tenders. Acting against this would alienate too many people in the party. Many prominent party members feared arrest and prosecution should their government dealings become public knowledge.

Second, the calls for policy reform challenged too many policy and ideological holy cows. Many party members continued to believe that the state should lead the economy. For them, the proposed reforms were simply an ideological bridge too far. They could not accept that labour laws or empowerment guidelines needed to be watered down, as this would strengthen the private sector relative to the state.

The small number of reformists within the party found they had very little power to break this dangerous cycle, and that their warnings were probably five years too late. Disgusted and disappointed, many left the ANC, with some finding new political homes in the DA – which had attracted almost a third of the votes in 2019. They were replaced by a new generation of ANC leaders whose economic radicalism was matched only by their corruption. They lived the lives of the rich and famous, but spouted revolutionary rhetoric. Many had close ties with the SACP, trade unions, various youth movements, career civil servants, and the black business lobby.

Under their leadership in the years between 2019 and 2024, the policy environment continued to gravitate in no particular direction at all. Some party members proposed that labour laws be tightened further, even as alarm bells sounded about rates of unemployment. There was a lot of rhetoric about the need for stricter black economic empowerment policies, even as the education system faltered. There were also calls for accelerated land reform – even as evidence emerged that most land reform projects had failed, thus helping to fuel food price hikes. Yet the threats and rhetoric seldom turned into actual policy and legislation. The party was too wracked by infighting and ideological confusion to act in a unified and effective way. Having lost its effective thinkers and leaders, it had lost the ability to make and implement effective policy.

Economic policy remained confused. The economy stagnated, with levels of GDP growth remaining below 3%. Investment slowed, and South Africa continued to lag behind the investment levels seen in most prominent emerging markets. The tax base also stagnated. The budget and current account deficits ballooned and South Africa faced being downgraded by international ratings agencies. The rand weakened further against major currencies.

Research showed that living standards had stagnated. Inflation eroded the real value of social welfare, which directly reduced the spending power of between a third and a half of all households. Levels of absolute poverty, which had declined during the first 20 years of democracy, flattened out and began to increase in some areas. The budget deficit precluded the accelerated roll-out of free and subsidised housing and electricity. Transport and energy costs increased in excess of the rate of inflation.

It was against this background that South Africans went to vote in 2024. The run-up to the election had seen a series of largely comical and inept attempts by the ANC to stifle the free flow of information and undermine the media, judiciary, and civil society. However, these were successfully challenged in the courts. It tried to restrict the activities of journalists, but this also failed due to court challenges as well as adverse public opinion. It also tried to manipulate the bench, but the independence of most judges, as well as their institutional memory, meant that the courts continued to safeguard the constitution. The government also sought to restrict sources of funding for civil society. But all these attempts fell flat, were never acted upon, or were set aside by the courts. Various dirty tricks campaigns – including trumped-up allegations of financial and other misconduct – were plotted against the leaders of opposition parties. However, these charges were easily exposed for what they were and, rather than weakening the targeted opposition leaders and parties, helped to further turn public opinion against the ANC.

A major problem for the ANC, and a key reason why its plotting and scheming failed, was that the party itself was coming apart at the seams. Leading members of the party spent more time fighting each other than dealing with external threats to their political future. When one internal faction criticised the media or the judiciary, another would turn on that faction in an effort to settle internal political scores.

It therefore came as no surprise when, in the 2024 elections, the ANC's share of the vote slipped by 10 percentage points to below 50%. Voters deserted it in large numbers in favour of a DA-led coalition of opposition parties, or stayed away from the polls. In a sight that had seemed unthinkable a decade earlier, the DA leader was sworn into office in front of the Union Buildings – standing where Nelson Mandela had stood 30 years previously. However, celebrations within the DA were short-lived as the party got down to the intimidating task of turning the economy around, and reversing the nation's fortunes.

More about the present

South Africa remains a tense and uncertain environment. Levels of poverty and inequality remain high, and the economy has yet to show signs of a sustained recovery. Despite the DA's victory, less than half of South Africans voted in 2024. Analysts are warning that, if the DA does not deliver in short order, a far more unpleasant political transition awaits. The danger here is very real. The ANC, stunned at losing an election, has fallen in with the radical left and now promises all kinds of populist policies if voters will give it just one more chance. The DA has a small parliamentary majority and the increasingly radical ANC could easily win the 2029 election.

Suburbs are showing the consequences of another decade of slow economic growth. Roads are potholed, and fewer traffic lights and street lights are working. Crime levels remain high and middle-class people rely on the private security industry, and poor communities on vigilantes, to safeguard their homes and families. Among other things, the DA now faces the difficult task of turning the ineffective and corrupt police force around.

The urban peripheries are littered with shacks and reveal the stark inequalities that still threaten to derail South Africa's post-1994 democracy. Half of young people are without work, and welfare remains a significant source of income for half of the country's households – even as inflation threatens to reduce the value of those social grants.

The DA also needs to turn around the public education system, which has deteriorated further over the past ten years. This is perhaps its most formidable challenge. Literacy and numeracy levels are languishing. Good teachers are in short supply, and allegations of drunkenness and sexual predation abound. The DA's task is complicated by the fact that the biggest teachers' union remains loyal to the ANC and has indicated that it will oppose any attempts by the DA to reform the schooling system.

The DA also needs to overcome further union hostility in order to reform the public service, which remains corrupt and incompetent. Government hospitals are in a state of decay, and the Department of Home Affairs is in turmoil. The former ANC-aligned civil service is hostile to the DA government. Many civil servants – particularly political appointees – do not trust the new ruling party, and fear they will lose their jobs.

The business and investment community is waiting for signs of what they may expect from the DA government and are alarmed at what they hear from the ANC opposition. They do not expect the corruption they encountered under the ANC but fear that a naive continued commitment to BEE and employment equity may scupper the DA's chances of drawing the investment they need to grow the economy and create jobs. They also fear what will happen if the DA loses its parliamentary majority in the 2029 election – and this uncertainty is delaying investment decisions.

The DA is faced with a major challenge since it has gained power on the back of promises to uphold the empowerment and redistribution policies of the ANC. However, many observers and analysts realise that these policies are inimical to growth and investment, and explain much of the demise of the ANC. If the DA persists with ANC-type policies, many believe it will suffer the fate of the ANC. Yet, to abandon those policies now would be to play into the hands, and the rhetoric, of the radical ANC opposition.

Despite the considerable odds, an outside chance remains that, if it succeeds in reforming economic policy, the DA government may still draw the investment levels, economic growth, and job creation needed to improve living standards, meet public expectations, and stay in power. But the radicals are knocking at the door and the DA's time in office will be short if it fails to dramatically improve the lives of all South Africans over the next five years.

Road map to this future

If we are headed for this future, you should be able to identify 80% or more of the route markers set out below. If you do not, you need to look at the route maps for the other three scenarios.

Tickbox for the Toll Road	✓
The ANC continues to blame everyone but itself for South Africa's social and economic problems.	◯

The ANC states publicly that it does not need to change and makes up all kinds of (often ridiculous) excuses for its corruption and incompetence.

◯

Infighting and ideological confusion characterise and weaken policy-making in the ANC.

◯

The DA hits the ANC hard on corruption and incompetence, while adopting more and more ANC policies, and even appropriating its heroes.

◯

The media casts an increasingly positive light on the DA and its policy proposals, while slating the government and the ANC.

◯

Civil society leads growing campaigns against the government and the ANC.

◯

The courts routinely find in favour of civil society in legal challenges to government policy.

◯

Efforts by the government to restrict the free flow of information and undermine the media and civil society activists do not succeed.

◯

Civil society, journalists, columnists, and opposition leaders routinely ridicule the ANC's efforts at restricting political freedoms and undermining democratic institutions.

◯

The political opposition is free to campaign.

◯

The DA directly targets former ANC supporters and secures the public support of some high-profile black leaders.

Economic growth dwindles for much of the decade to 2024.

Investment and savings levels remain unchanged, or drop further.

The unemployment rate remains around 25%.

Inflation exceeds its target zone, as the rand weakens further.

Public protests continue to escalate.

Inflation erodes the real value of social grants.

The budget deficit continues to grow, thus undermining the government's ability to sustain its functions and services.

People on welfare continue to outnumber those with formal jobs.

The roll-out of free houses, electricity, and water begins to slow.

Public services continue to decline, and many areas are without water and electricity for days on end.

The government blames sinister forces for seeking to destabilise the country.

The government blames business and investors for slow economic growth and high levels of unemployment.

The ANC's more pragmatic leaders leave the party and the government.

The government tries to tighten BEE and employment equity policy, accelerate land reform, and tighten labour laws, but makes little actual progress.

Property rights are threatened.

OUR ROUTE TO
THE FUTURE

Many attempts have been made to predict the future of a country or economy. While some forecasters have been lucky, most economists, political analysts and researchers have come to realise that this is a futile exercise. Some have given up. Others continue to flounder around trying to guess at the future, despite all their previous failures.

A smaller band of analysts has come to understand that scenarios offer a very effective way of gaining insight into the futures of the countries and economies they are studying. They know that the futures of such complex systems are inherently unpredictable, and are shaped by a wide range of factors that can combine in many different ways to produce very different outcomes. However, they also know that it is possible to identify the major forces that are propelling those systems into the future, and that those drivers can be used to plot a plausible set of alternative futures within which the actual future will eventually fall. Put differently – those forces provide us with highways to the future. By reading the route markers along the way it is possible to develop an accurate sense of which future will be realised.

I previously mentioned the example of the CIA deriding a Shell scenario detailing the demise of the Soviet Union and the end of the Cold War. Less than five years later, Ronald Reagan stood in front of the Brandenburg Gate and told his Soviet counterpart, Mikhail Gorbachev, to 'tear down this wall'. Shortly thereafter the Soviet Union had disintegrated, and the Cold War – which had dominated global politics for more than 40 years – had ended.

Likewise, we cited the South African example of PW Botha telling the world in August 1985 that South Africa would not be dictated to, and would not reform. Within five years, his party had dismantled apartheid, and within five more years Nelson Mandela was sworn in as president. Just ten years later, the last leader of the National Party, Marthinus 'Kortbroek' van Schalkwyk (known as 'Sonderbroek' in the Free State as a reference to his changing political convictions), was serving as Minister of Tourism in an ANC government.

We now have the advantage of knowing what Cold War and apartheid era analysts did not know, namely why and how the world changes. We know that very small, almost insignificant, changes in the present political and economic conditions of any country or economy can bring about huge shifts in its future. We also know that these small changes are the result of feedback from ordinary people, politicians, business people, journalists, and civil society leaders in an effort to preserve or change the status quo. Drawing further on complex systems theory, we have characterised this as the butterfly effect. The changes that amazed and surprised people in Russia, the United States, and South Africa were actually not that amazing. What was described as a miracle in South Africa's case was simply a function of this powerful, but unseen, effect at work.

Instead of trying to forecast a single future, then, one should allow for the butterfly effect, and plot a range of different futures. This can be done by identifying the most important trends in the current system – known as key driving forces or trend highways – and working out how they could interact with one another. If we accurately identify those driving forces, and plot them well against each other, they present us with a spectrum of futures for the country or economy being studied. These scenarios are not forecasts; they are meant to be equally plausible, and scenario planners do not predict at the outset that we will wind up in one of those futures. However, taken together, a well-built set of scenarios does present us with the outer boundaries of the future, and we will land up somewhere within their confines.

In South Africa's case, our scenarios show that economic policy decisions taken over the next ten years, together with the maintenance or otherwise of democratic freedoms and the rule of law, will play vital roles in shaping our future. Using these two variables as the axes of a matrix, we wound up with four scenario wire frames. We then used all the other driving forces – as well as relatively permanent features of South African society – to flesh out those wire frames into fully fledged descriptions of the future.

When economic reforms are combined with restrictions on democratic rights and freedoms, we wind up in the Narrow Road scenario. In this future, the country will be more politically stable and also more prosperous than it is today. In material terms, life will be better, for the rich as well as the poor. However, we will be less free to vote, protest, strike, or criticise the government. It is therefore a future in which we sacrifice liberty in favour of prosperity. It is the exact opposite of our current society, which is very free but also very poor and unequal, with an underperforming economy.

You and your family could easily find yourself in this future within a decade. If you are a member of the (traditionally largely white but increasingly multiracial) middle class, probably living in a suburb, you would have a good and well-paid job, be able to practise your profession, or be able to run a profitable business. Your children would be well educated, and would also find work. Your neighbourhood would be safer. However, your newspaper and the evening SABC news might not tell you the whole truth about current affairs, and besides voting once in every five years you would not have much scope for expressing your political views.

If you are a member of the (traditionally largely black) working class, or the new class of the permanently unemployed, living in a former township or informal settlement, and perhaps subsisting on social grants, your material outlook would also be significantly improved. For the first time in many years, you might be able to find a job. Your children's education in local government schools would improve, and they, too, would have a better chance of finding work. Your living standards might improve, and you might have a chance to actively shape your own future instead of relying on social welfare. If you go on strike, though, or join a service delivery protest, you are likely to face harsh police action.

Many South Africans might be prepared to settle for this future. However, an even greater prize awaits us in the form of the Wide Road scenario. This is what would happen to us if the government implements those same economic reforms without undermining democratic freedoms. Instead of trying to force through initially unpopular economic reforms by suppressing people's means to express themselves democratically, it uses democratic institutions to sell the benefits of reform to citizens, thereby winning their long-term support for further reforms. In this future, the economy would also grow more rapidly, and more people would find work. South Africa would attract more investment, and many more businesses would be established. Living standards would improve significantly, and levels of inequality would diminish. The difference here would be that democracy is consolidated, and civil liberties are respected – in other words, that South Africans remain free while they are also becoming more prosperous.

Again, you might well find yourself living in this country in ten years' time. If you are a member of the middle class, your children would still be well educated, and would pursue successful careers. You should be wealthier, and living in greater comfort. Safety would remain a concern. Your lifestyle could still revolve around rugby or soccer, shopping malls, going to movies, and having braais next to your swimming pool. You would be well informed by a free and vigorous media, which would play a constructive watchdog role. Besides voting for a party of your choice once every five years, you would be able to freely express your views in a number of different ways, build or participate in political organisations, and participate in civil society organisations.

If you are a member of the working class, or the class of the unemployed, your life would also improve significantly. Your economic prospects would improve, similar to those in the previous scenario. Besides voting for and participating in the party of your choice, you would be able to actively participate in public life via vigorous civil society organisations, and freely take part in legal strikes and protests.

However, while things could get better than they are today, they could also get much worse. The worst-case scenario will arise if the government does not introduce economic reforms, and also tears down democratic institutions and civil liberties in an attempt to restrict or suppress public dissent and remain in power. This is the Rocky Road, and, while we may not like to think about it, it is as plausible as any of the others. In this future, economic growth would plummet. Our society would be poorer as well as even more unequal. Political instability would return to the levels seen in the last decade of apartheid South Africa. Journalists would be detained, and civil society organisations banned.

If you are a member of the middle classes and run a business, let alone a farm, start making plan B, because you are going to need it. The value of your investments will be eroded or destroyed. Make sure your children are educated to a level where they can find work elsewhere in Africa or overseas.

Build relationships with distant foreign relatives, as you may need them to bail you out. Expect your living standards to deteriorate and that you will increasingly need to assume responsibility for your own water and electricity supply. Expect your children to emigrate if they can, and be prepared to support their decision. Do not expect to speak your mind in public, even in the face of the most outrageous corruption and human rights abuses. You would not want to be caught in this scenario because you might well find you have no way out.

This is doubly true if you are a member of the working class or the army of the unemployed. The value of the social grants that help you to feed your family will be eroded as food and transport prices escalate. In this instance, you will also be politically emasculated. You will be 'encouraged' to vote for the ruling party, and intimidated if you do not. If you work for an activist civil society organisation, go on strike, or take part in a community protest, you could wind up in jail. Unlike members of the middle class, you will have no practical prospects of leaving the country and building a life elsewhere.

However, once again this future is not inevitable, and we might well land up in our fourth scenario, namely the Toll Road. The economy continues to underperform, while demands on the government continue to rise. As a result of ineptitude and infighting, the ANC fails in its bid to destroy the constitution, which remains strong. Expect ten years of poor economic growth, culminating in an ANC electoral defeat in 2024. This will introduce the unfamiliar sight of a DA president in the Union Buildings. It is unclear, though, whether the DA will be able to reform the civil service and implement policies that will succeed where the ANC failed. Levels of unemployment will remain very high and violent community protests will continue.

If you are a member of the middle classes, expect that in real terms your living standards have stagnated or declined. Expect that the streets in your neighbourhoods are badly kept and littered with potholes. Public services are poor and you have put up with ten years of worsening corruption. If your children are not in a good suburban school, or an expensive private school, you have a problem. Standards at universities have fallen and your children need to access scholarships to foreign institutions. Get little Johnny to practise his kicking. The United States will be an increasingly serious contender in the Rugby World Cup, and many scholarships will be on offer for South Africans to play rugby at American universities. If a sustained global economic recovery coincides with this scenario, expect growing demand for your skills in Europe, Asia, North America, and the Middle East. Also look to Africa which may by now be growing rapidly enough to offer the economic opportunities that South Africa no longer does. If you do not avail yourself of these opportunities, your streets will remain dangerous, and poverty and desperation will confront you wherever you go. However, you will still have a measure of protection behind high walls and electric fences.

If you are a member of the working class, or the huge class of endemically unemployed, your situation will also be far worse. You will probably not have a job – and certainly not a good, stable, and well-paid one. Your welfare income will be eroded by inflation. Levels of crime in your area will remain high. You will still be able to vote, and take part in strikes or political protests, but these will only lead to a second, more violent, revolution if the DA government fails to gain traction.

I am often asked which of these futures I believe will come to pass. My answer is that the butterfly effect means that any of them could materialise. To assign probabilities to any of these scenarios would turn them into forecasts. This would also contradict the complex systems basis of this book, which holds that small changes in a current system could bring about very large changes in the future. After all, this is the reason why *not one* of the major shifts in economic or political systems during the past 100 years was forecast with any degree of accuracy. Also, if one scenario is taken to be more probable than another, fixating on that scenario may cause end users to overlook evidence that another scenario is becoming more plausible.

Seeking absolute certainty about the future is dangerous. It is impossible to achieve, no matter how good your analysts or your data. It is also futile. Rather accept that the future is inherently uncertain, and that you need to build some highways, and identify the road signs along those highways, to navigate your way into 2024 with any degree of precision. For example, in South Africa today many people may feel that scenarios involving economic stagnation and democratic decline are more plausible than those involving reform and prosperity. It is certainly true that short-term trends point towards stagnation and decline. However, take yourself back to the night of the Rubicon speech, and the danger inherent in fixating on short-terms trends becomes apparent.

For this reason, I sincerely believe a reform scenario is

plausible, as is the stability and prosperity this will bring. Therefore, do not write off the current ruling party – it can still change the country for the better if reformers in its ranks gain control of the party and its policy decisions. By the same token, it is quite possible that the DA could occupy the Union Buildings within a decade.

I am also at pains to point out to clients that scenarios are not fixed, box-like outcomes. We must not expect to wind up in precisely one box or another. Perhaps the best quote about scenarios is one by Stewart Brand that appears on the back of Peter Schwartz's excellent book *The Art of the Long View,* namely that scenarios 'ensure that you are not always right about the future – but better – that you are almost never wrong about the future'. Therefore, while our actual future may fall roughly within the confines of a particular scenario, it may not reach its limits. For example, despite failing to reform the economy and boost economic growth, the ANC might hang on by the skin of its teeth for one more election post 2024. However, give or take a few years, and a few points of economic growth and inflation, and these scenarios provide us with an accurate map of what will happen over the next ten years.

When I was first approached to write this book I insisted that it had to be a practical guide to the future written as much for an ordinary family worried about their future in our country as for the concerned CEO in Sandton or professional policy analyst in Washington – and I hope that I have gone some way towards meeting this challenge. The most practical thing you can do now in making decisions about your future is to read and understand the road signs. I have already listed some of those road signs, and you may identify others I have missed. Some of these may be unique to your business or personal circumstances. Some of these will be in your face, and unmissable. Yet others will be more obscure. Some may never materialise, and if they do they may not be noticed.

Economic policy reforms and the growth of a reform movement within the ANC are vital route markers, and should be easy to follow. Should the government relax labour market controls as well as BEE and employment equity requirements, we will be well on our way to the Wide Road and Narrow Road scenarios. Should the government remain in denial about the state of the economy, or suggest that it can lead higher levels of growth through nationalisation and greater state participation, we are heading for the Rocky Road or the Toll Road. In this context, economic route markers and warning signs include:

- **The future of COSATU and the SACP.** Should they withdraw from the tripartite alliance, or be forced out by the ANC, the country will be heading towards the Wide Road or Narrow Road. Should COSATU and the SACP capture the alliance and start filling more cabinet posts, expect the opposite to happen.
- **Inflation targeting.** Should inflation targeting be maintained, this will mean the ANC reformists have retained control of the alliance. Should it be abandoned, this will signal that they have lost control, and we are heading towards a more adverse future.
- **Changes in ANC leadership.** Should leading and respected figures in key economic and financial

government posts resign, and perhaps leave the party, this will point towards the Rocky Road and Toll Road. This will also hold true if radical youth leaders expelled from the ANC Youth League, or now in the EFF, are welcomed back into the party.

- **The state of the economy.** Should the rate of growth reach 5% of GDP, we will definitely be in Wide Road or Narrow Road territory. Should growth continue to languish below 3% of GDP, this will be a warning sign that we are heading towards the other scenarios.
- **Savings and fixed investment rates.** If these pick up to emerging market norms, we are heading for the Wide Road or Narrow Road. If they dwindle at current levels, or drop further, we are heading for a far less favourable economic future.
- **Unemployment levels.** Similarly, if formal unemployment levels remain at 25% or higher, or the labour market absorption rate falls further, we are in Rocky Road or Toll Road territory. However, should unemployment fall to below 20%, this will indicate that we are swinging towards their more positive counterparts.
- **The rate of inflation.** Given the way in which high rates of inflation weaken household income and living standards – thus undermining social welfare – rampant inflation will be a key warning sign that we have turned towards the Rocky Road or Toll Road.
- **The budget deficit.** If this rises above 5% of GDP, especially in a low growth environment, this will mean that the government is running out of money, and we are again on our way towards a more adverse future.

- **The state of public education.** If the number of good maths passes in matric starts rising, this will indicate that we are heading for more skills, more productive employment, and higher growth levels, all taking us towards the Wide Road and Narrow Road. Conversely, should the performance of the public schooling system continue to languish at current levels, or deteriorate even further, this will be a major warning sign that we are heading into danger.

Political route markers and warning signs include:

- **Democratic rights and freedoms.** If the government tries to erode these rights and freedoms, we are heading for the Narrow Road or Rocky Road, depending on how far the government is prepared to go. However should this not happen, the constitution be respected, and political and civil liberties be entrenched, we are heading for the Wide Road or Toll Road, depending on whether the government implements the correct economic policy reforms.
- **Property rights.** If these are maintained, this will help us to steer clear of the Rocky Road.
- **Media freedom.** Free media will help to guide us onto the Wide Road or Toll Road. Conversely, if the government acts to curb the media, this will push us towards the other two scenarios.
- **The state of civil society.** Should civil society remain active, and free and unregulated, this will help to

guide us towards the Wide Road or Toll Road. Should the government attempt to restrict civil society, and its ability to challenge the state, it will close off those routes and divert us towards the Narrow Road or Rocky Road instead.

There are many other smaller road signs, including actual road signs and working traffic lights, that will be very good indicators of where South Africa is headed. As long as these are maintained, we are heading for the Wide Road or Narrow Road. If the police are friendly and helpful, we are most probably on our way to the Wide Road scenario. But, if police officers abuse their power and are violent without cause, then the Toll Road or Rocky Road most likely beckons. Likewise, if the civil servants you encounter at government offices are corrupt, discourteous and lazy, this will suggest that we are headed for the Toll Road or the Rocky Road.

From this point forward, keeping track of our progress into the future will depend on your ability to read the route markers and warning signs on our highways to the future. If you do this well, you will know what your life in a future South Africa will be like long before you have the experience of actually living it.

Therefore, the challenge that confronts us is to do everything in our power to realise the best-case scenario and avoid the worst.

ENDNOTES

CHAPTER 1

1   Television address to the nation by ANC President Nelson Mandela on the assassination of Chris Hani, 13 April 1993, http://www.anc.org.za/show.php?id=4304.
2   Wilson, I: "From Scenario Thinking to Strategic Action", *Horizon*, 2000, http://horizon.unc.edu/projects/seminars/futurizing/action.asp.
3   IRR: *South Africa Survey 2008/2009*, Johannesburg, 2009, pp. 91-92.
4   Ibid., p. 89.
5   IRR: *South Africa Survey 2010/2011*, Johannesburg, 2011, p. 121.
6   IRR: *South Africa Survey 2008/2009*, Johannesburg, 2009 p. 120.
7   Ibid., p. 135.
8   IRR: *South Africa Survey 2009/2010*, Johannesburg, 2010 p. 150.
9   IRR: *South Africa Survey 2008/2009*, Johannesburg, 2009 p. 170.
10 Ibid., p. 173.
11 IRR: *South Africa Survey 2013*, Johannesburg, 2013, p. 647.
12 Ibid., p. 229.
13 IRR: *South Africa Survey 2013*, Johannesburg, 2013, pp. 610, 590.
14 IRR: *South Africa Survey 2012*, Johannesburg, 2012, p. 303.
15 IRR: *82nd Annual Report*, Johannesburg, July 2012, p. 22, http://www.sairr.org.za/profile/annual-report/Web.2011-12%20Annual%20Report.11Jun12.pdf/view.
16 IRR: *South Africa Survey 2010/2011*, Johannesburg, 2011 pp. 130-131.
17 Ibid., p. 115.
18 Medium term budget policy speech – Pravin Gordhan, *Politicsweb*, 25 October 2012, http://www.politicsweb.co.za/politicsweb/view/politicsweb/en/page72308?oid=335383&sn=Detail&pid=72308.
19 Economic and Financial Indicators, published online by *The Economist*, http://www.economist.com/category/print-sections/economic-and-financial-indicators.
20 Global Investment Trends Monitor, published online by the United Nations Conference on Trade and Development (UNCTAD), No. 10, 23 October 2012, http://unctad.org/en/PublicationsLibrary/webdiaeia2012d20_en.pdf.
21 I-Net Bridge, "Marcus: Weaker rand key inflation risk," *Business Report*, 4 July 2012, http://m.br.co.za/article/view/s/28/a/253379.
22 "Overview of the South African economy," address by G Marcus, governor of the

South African Reserve Bank at the 93rd ordinary general meeting of shareholders, Pretoria, 26 July 2013, http://www.bis.org/review/r130802d.pdf.

23   Mogotsi, I: "Jacob Zuma: Strong on affability, weak on policy", *Politicsweb*, 30 October 2012, http://www.politicsweb.co.za/politicsweb/view/politicsweb/en/page71619?oid=336564&sn=Marketingweb+detail.

24   The New Growth Path: The Framework, 23 November 2010, http://www.info.gov.za/speeches/docs/2010/new-growth-path.pdf.

25   National Development Plan, 11 November 2011, http://www.npconline.co.za/medialib/downloads/home/NPC%20National%20Development%20Plan%20Vision%202030%20-lo-res.pdf.

26   IRR: *South Africa Survey 2008/2009*, Johannesburg, 2009, pp. 222, 236.

27   IRR: *South Africa Survey 2010/2011*, Johannesburg, 2011, p. 254.

28   IRR: *South Africa Survey 2013*, Johannesburg, 2013, p. 344.

29   Ibid., p. 321.

30   Filen, C: "Miners need to tackle unemployment ticking time-bomb – Shabangu", *MineWeb*, 5 June 2012, http://www.mineweb.com/mineweb/content/en/mineweb-political-economy?oid=152725&sn=Detail&pid=102055.

31   Hlubi, P: 'Unemployment a ticking time bomb – Vavi', *Eyewitness News*, 16 May 2012, http://ewn.co.za/2012/05/16/Poor-rage-against-rich-growing-Vavi.

32   Mbeki, M: "Wealth creation", *Business Day Live*, 10 February 2011, http://www.bdlive.co.za/articles/2011/02/10/wealth-creation;jsessionid=3D0F897F05EBAC5E33DE341F908680E3.present1.bdfm.

33   Kane-Berman, J: "South Africa in 2012: Tipping Point or Turning Point", address at IRR South Africa Mirror Briefing, Johannesburg Country Club, 21 November 2012.

34   Speech by FW de Klerk to a private meeting in Johannesburg, 31 October 2012.

35   AFP: "Motlanthe fires warning at ANC", *iafrica.com*, 15 July 2013, http://news.iafrica.com/sa/870354.html.Bottom of Form.

36   Bryce-Pease, S: "Lack of service delivery could cost ANC its majority", SABC News, 23 July 2013, http://www.sabc.co.za/news/a/1342440040752ea38327832154f093f8/Lack-of-service-delivery-could-cost-ANC-its-majority:-Mlangeni-20132307.

37   IRR: *South Africa Survey 2008/2009*, Johannesburg, 2009, pp. 718-719.

38   Alexander, P: "Protests and police statistics in South Africa: Some commentary", *Leninology*, 3 April 2012, http://www.leninology.com/2012/04/protests-and-police-statistics-some.html.

39   Sapa: "Political killings: A timeline", *Metro Newspaper*, 2 August 2012, http://www.metronewspaper.co.za/2012/08/02/political-killings-a-timeline/.

40   Alexander, P: "Protests and police statistics in South Africa".

41   England, A: "Moody's downgrades South Africa", *Financial Times*, 27 September 2012, http://www.ft.com/cms/s/0/5a49505a-08c0-11e2-9176-00144feabdc0.html#axzz2kbB83abW.

42   Author unknown: "Cry, the beloved country", *The Economist*, 20 October 2012, http://www.economist.com/news/leaders/21564846-south-africa-sliding-downhill-while-much-rest-continent-clawing-its-way-up.

43   Sunter, C: "The world and South Africa beyond 2012: The latest scenarios, flags

and probabilities and their implications for health care", speech to IRR event at the Johannesburg Country Club, 28 June 2012.

44 Schwartz, P: *The Art of the Long View: Planning for the Future in an Uncertain World.* California: Doubleday, 1991, p. 202.

CHAPTER 2

1   Ringland, G: *Scenario Planning: Managing for the Future.* England: John Wiley & Sons, 2006, pp. 14-15.

2   Kennedy, P, Perrottet, C and Thomas, C: "Scenario planning after 9/11: Managing the impact of a catastrophic event", *Strategy and Leadership*, 31(1), 2003, pp. 4-5.

3   Schwartz, P: *The Art of the Long View:* p. 55.

4   Ralston, WK and Wilson, I: *Scenario Planning Handbook: Developing Strategies in Uncertain Times.* Ohio: Thompson, 2006, p. 3.

5   The idea was first introduced by the mathematician and meteorologist Edward Lorenz, and then taken up in chaos theory.

6   See, for example, Marren, PB and Kennedy, PJ Jr, "Scenario planning for economic recovery: Short-term decision-making in a recession", *Strategy and Leadership*, 38(1), p. 11; Schoemaker, PJH: "Scenario planning: A tool for strategic thinking", *Sloan Management Review*, 36(2), p. 25, and Van der Merwe, L: "Scenario-based strategy in practice: A framework", *Advances in Developing Human Resources*, 10(2), p. 218.

7   This result would later converge very well with thinking that underpinned the rise of scenario planning.

8   Courtney, H: *20/20 Foresight: Crafting Strategy in an Uncertain World.* Boston: Harvard Business School Press, 2001, pp. 16-20.

9   Ralston, WK and Wilson, I: *Scenario Planning Handbook*, pp. 3-4.

10 Wack, P: "Scenarios: Uncharted waters ahead", *Harvard Business Review*, 63(5), 1985, p. 73.

11 Schnaars, SP: "The essentials of scenario writing", *Industrial Marketing Management*, 28(6), 1999, p. 7; Millet, SM: "The future of scenarios: Challenges and opportunities", *Strategy and Leadership*, 31(2), p. 17; Ringland, G: *Scenario Planning*, p. 13; Schwartz, P: *The Art of the Long View*, p. 7.

12 Millet, SM: "The future of scenarios", p. 17; Ringland, G: *Scenario Planning*, p. 13.

13 Van der Heijden, K: *Scenarios: The Art of Strategic Conversation.* England: John Wiley & Sons, 2005, p. 3.

14 See http://www.megadeth.com/faq and http://en.wikipedia.org/wiki/Megadeth.

15 Millet, SM: "The future of scenarios", p. 17.

16 Ringland, G: *Scenario Planning*, pp. 14-16.

17 Wack, P: "Scenarios", pp. 73-77; Ringland, G: *Scenario Planning*, pp. 20-22.

18 Van der Heijden, K: *Scenarios*, p. 5.

19 Wack, P: "Scenarios", pp. 73-77.

20 Ringland, G: *Scenario Planning*, pp. 20-22.

21 Schwartz, P: *The Art of the Long View*, pp. 7-9.

22 Van der Heijden, K: *Scenarios*, p. 5.

23 Wack, P: "Scenarios", pp. 73-74.

24   Schwartz, P: *The Art of the Long View,* pp. 7-9.

25   Ringland, G: *Scenario Planning,* p. 21.

26   Ibid.; Schwartz, P: *The Art of the Long View*, pp. 7-9.

27   Van der Heijden, K: *Scenarios*, p. 6.

28   Ringland, G: *Scenario Planning*, p. 180.

29   Van der Heijden, K: *Scenarios*, p. 18.

CHAPTER 3

1   Ringland, G: *Scenario Planning*, p. 7.

2   Van der Heijden, K: *Scenarios,* p. 6.

3   Marren, PB and Kennedy, PJ Jr: "Scenario planning for economic recovery: Short-term decision-making in a recession", *Strategy and Leadership*, 38(1), p. 11; Saunders, SG: "Scenario Planning: A collage construction approach", *Foresight*, 11(2), 2009, p. 19; Fontela, E: "Fore Front: Bridging the gap between scenarios and models", *Foresight*, 2(1), p. 11.

4   Ralston, WK and Wilson, I: *Scenario Planning Handbook,* pp. 16-19.

5   Ibid.

6   Ibid., p. 4.

7   Wack, P: "Scenarios", p. 73.

8   This approach draws heavily on Peter Schwartz's excellent book *The Art of the Long View: Planning for the Future in an Uncertain World*, which is essential reading for anyone wishing to better understand scenarios and how to build them.

9   Schwartz, P: *The Art of the Long View,* pp. 243-248.

CHAPTER 4

1   IRR: *South Africa Survey 2013*, Johannesburg, 2013, p. 265.

2   Ibid., pp. 234-235.

3   Ibid., p. 237.

4   Ibid., p. 328.

5   World Bank, GINI index, 2012, http://data.worldbank.org/indicator/SI.POV.GINI.

6   IRR: *South Africa Survey 2013*, Johannesburg, 2013, p. 342.

7   Ibid., pp. 180-185.

8   Ibid., pp. 3-12, 241.

9   Cervantes, M, McMahon, F and Wilson, A: *Survey of Mining Companies 2012/2013*. Canada: Fraser Institute, 2013, p. 14.

10   Seccombe, A: "Nationalisation scary, so drop the word – Cutifani", *Business Day*, 10 October 2011.

11   Shoba, S: "Mboweni scathing on 'reckless' nationalism row" *Business Day*, 18 July 2011.

12   Scholtz, J: "Attorneys agree court is a mess", *Business Day*, 12 November 2010.

13   Gorton, B: "What I want to see in a political party", *Sunday Times*, 12 June 2012.

14   Prinsloo, L: "SA school system not producing the skills needed – PMI", *Engineering News*, 20 January 2011.

15   Brendan Boyle: "The blueprint for a new economy", *Sunday Times*, 27 November 2005.

16 IRR: *South Africa Survey 2013*, Johannesburg, 2013, p. 136.

17 United Nations Conference on Trade and Development (UNCTAD): *Global Investment Trends Monitor*, www.unctad.org.

18 Haldenwang, B: *Projections of the South African Population, 1985-2040 (with AIDS and no AIDS projections)*. Cape Town: Institute for Futures Research, 2011, p. 2; IRR: *South Africa Survey 2010/2011*, Johannesburg, 2011, p. 52.

19 IRR: *South Africa Survey 2013*, Johannesburg, 2013, pp. 59-64.

20 Feinstein, A: *After the Party: A Personal and Political Journey inside the ANC*. Johannesburg: Jonathan Ball, 2007, p. 249.

21 IRR: *South Africa Survey 2010/2011*, Johannesburg, 2011, p. 560.

22 IRR: *South Africa Survey 2013*, Johannesburg, 2013, p. 470.

23 "South Africa in 2024", briefing prepared by Frans Cronje for clients of the Centre for Risk Analysis; IRR: *South Africa Survey 2013*, Johannesburg, 2013, p. 518.

24 IRR: *South Africa Survey 2009/2010*, Johannesburg, 2010, pp. 422-423.

25 IRR: *South Africa Survey 2013*, Johannesburg, 2013, pp. 540-550.

26 Ibid., p. 470.

27 Ibid., p. 256.

28 IRR: *South Africa Survey 2010/2011*, Johannesburg, 2011, p. 273.

29 Estimate by FirstRand economists.

30 IRR: *South Africa Survey 2013*, Johannesburg, 2013, p. 668.

31 IRR: *South Africa Survey 2012*, Johannesburg, 2012, p. 583; National Treasury: *Estimates of National Expenditure*. Pretoria, 2001, http://www.treasury.gov.za/documents/national%20budget/2001/ene/foreword.pdf.

32 IRR: *South Africa Survey 2010/2011*, Johannesburg, 2011, p. 761; United Nations Office on Drugs and Crime: *Eleventh United National Survey of Crime Trends and Operations of Criminal Justice Systems 2003-2008*, Vienna, 2008, https://www.unodc.org/unodc/en/data-and-analysis/crime_survey_eleventh.html.

33 IRR: *South Africa Survey 2010/2011*, Johannesburg, 2011, p. 809.

34 IRR: *South Africa Survey 2012*, Johannesburg, 2012, p. 811.

35 Ibid., p. 697.

36 IRR: *South Africa Survey 2010/2011*, Johannesburg, 2011, p. 831.

37 IRR: *South Africa Survey 2012*, Johannesburg, 2012, p. 662; OMD South Africa and AdReview: *South Africa and SADC Media Facts 2011*, Johannesburg, 2011, http://www.omd.co.za/media_facts/samediafacts2011.pdf.

38 Sapa: "Court rules in AfriForum's favour that all Pta schools' power supply must be restored", *Link2Media*, 18 September 2009, http://www.link2media.co.za/index.php?option=com_content&task=view&id=5639&Itemid=15.

39 Mabuza, E: "Zuma loses appeal on Zimbabwe report", *Business Day*, 15 December 2010.

40 Author unknown: "CSA wins bid for travelgate records", *Saturday Star*, 29 July 2011.

41 Author unknown: "Rare unified voice against the Info Bill", *Business Day*, 23 November 2011.

42 Author unknown: "It's the citizens' right to appeal to the con court", *The Star*, 15 September 2011.

43 Constitution of the Republic of South Africa, Act 108 of 1996, Chapter 2, Section 9, http://www.gov.za/documents/constitution/1996/a108-96.pdf.

44 Jeffery, A: *Chasing the Rainbow: South Africa's Move from Mandela to Zuma.* Johannesburg; IRR: 2010, p. 95.

45 Constitution of the Republic of South Africa, Chapter 2, Sections 15-19.

46 Jeffery, A: *Chasing the Rainbow*, p. 85.

47 Habib, A and De Vos, CM: "Human Rights", in *Public Attitudes in Contemporary South Africa.* Cape Town: HSRC Press, 2002, pp. 152-153.

48 Constitution of the Republic of South Africa, Chapter 2, Section 25.

49 Ibid., Sections 26-29.

50 Ibid., Sections 34, 35.

51 Jeffery, A: *Chasing the Rainbow*, p. 89.

52 IRR: *South Africa Survey 2012*, Johannesburg, 2012, p. 799.

53 Author unknown: "Litmus test for a young democracy", *City Press*, 19 February 2012.

54 Jeffery, A: *Chasing the Rainbow*, pp. 110-111.

55 Constitution of the Republic of South Africa, Chapter 9, Section 188.

56 Ibid., Section 182.

57 South African Human Rights Commission, *Annual Report 2012*. Johannesburg, 2012, http://www.sahrc.org.za/home/21/files/SAHRC%202012%2012%20Sept.pdf.

58 Phakathi, B: "DA gave 'Hobson's choice' on open toilets", *Business Day*, 27 October 2010.

59 Sapa: "JSC may look for consensus on Hlophe", *Sunday Independent*, 6 April 2011.

60 De Lange, D and Pietersen, M: "Judges lash Zuma", *The Star*, 2 December 2011.

CHAPTER 5

1 White Paper on Reconstruction and Development: Government's Strategy for Fundamental Transformation, November 1994, http://www.info.gov.za/view/downloadfileaction?id=70427.

2 Author and headline unknown, *The Star*, 31 August 1995.

3 Manuel, T: "RDP macroeconomic goals complement one another", *Business Day*, 28 October 1996.

4 Ibid.

5 Author and headline unknown, *Business Day*, 6 October 1994.

6 Author and headline unknown, *Business Day*, 22 September 1994.

7 Growth, Employment and Redistribution: A Macroeconomic Strategy, 14 June 1996, http://www.treasury.gov.za/publications/other/gear/chapters.pdf.

8 Author unknown, "ANC faithful embrace the free market", *Sunday Independent*, 21 December 1997.

9 ANC: "50th National Conference: Resolutions – Role of State and Governance", Mafikeng, 1997, http://www.anc.org.za/show.php?id=2425.

10 In the five years from 1994 to 1999, the economy grew by a mere 3.2%, 3.1%, 4.3%, 2.6%, 0.5%, and 2.4% respectively. IRR: *South Africa Survey 2012*, Johannesburg, 2012, pp. 105-106.

11 Ibid., p. 321.

12 IRR: *South Africa Survey 2010/21011*, Johannesburg, 2011, pp. 254-256.

13 Author and headline unknown, *Business Day*, 24 July 1996.

14 Author unknown: "Gear is the means for implementing the RDP, *Business Day*, 23 December 1997.

15 Phahlane, C: "SACP moves to play down shock attack by Mandela", *Business Day*, 2 July 1998.

16 Author and headline unknown, *Business Day*, 1 November 2001.

17 ANC: "51st National Conference: Resolutions", Stellenbosch, 20 December 2002, http://www.anc.org.za/show.php?id=2495.

18 Jeffery, A: *Chasing the Rainbow*, pp. 7, 15, 30, 127, 195, 249.

19 Mineral and Petroleum Resources Development Act, 2002, *Government Gazette*, 10 October 2002, http://www.info.gov.za/view/DownloadFileAction?id=68062.

20 Author and headline unknown, *Business Day*, 26 April 2002.

21 From 2000 to 2003 South Africa recorded GDP growth of 4.2%, 2.7%, 3.7%, and 2.9%. IRR: *South Africa Survey 2012*, Johannesburg, 2012, pp. 103-105.

22 IRR: *South Africa Survey 2010/2011*, Johannesburg, 2011, pp. 254-257.

23 Ibid., p. 310.

24 Accelerated and Shared Growth Initiative for South Africa (AsgiSA), 2006, http://www.info.gov.za/asgisa/asgisa.htm.

25 Media briefing by deputy president Phumzile Mlambo-Ngcuka, Parliamentary Monitoring Group, 6 February 2006, http://www.pmg.org.za/bills/060206asgisummary.htm.

26 Brown, K and Musgrave, A: "South Africa: ANC economic policy under fire", *Business Day*, 22 September 2006.

27 ANC: "52nd National Conference: Resolutions", Polokwane, 20 December 2007, http://www.anc.org.za/show.php?id=2536.

28 ANC: "ANC 2009 Manifesto: Working together we can do more", 2009, http://www.anc.org.za/docs/manifesto/2009/manifesto.pdf.

29 The economy had grown by 5.3%, 5.6%, 5.6%, and 3.6% since 2004, as South Africa capitalised on the tail-end of the global commodity boom. IRR: *South Africa Survey 2012*, Johannesburg, 2012, p. 104.

30 Ibid., p. 254.

31 Ibid., p. 171.

32 IRR: *South Africa Survey 2009/2010*, Johannesburg, 2010, p. 578; StatsSA: *General Household Survey* 2010, Pretoria, 2010, http://www.statssa.gov.za/publications/P0318/P0318April2012.pdf.

33 IRR: *South Africa Survey 2009/2010*, Johannesburg, 2010, p. 526.

34 IRR: *South Africa Survey 2012*, Johannesburg, 2012, p. 321.

35 Ibid., pp. 132-133.

36 Ibid.

37 Ibid., p. 104.

38 IRR: *South Africa Survey 2010/2011*, Johannesburg, 2011, p. 256.

39 The New Growth Path: The Framework, November 2011, http://www.info.gov.za/view/DownloadFileAction?id=135748.

40   Our Future: Make It Work, National Development Plan 2030. National Planning Commission, http://www.info.gov.za/view/DownloadFileAction?id=172297.

41   Laubscher, J: "Blueprint could fly", *Financial Mail,* 23 December 2011.

CHAPTER 6

1   National and provincial election results (archive for all elections since 1994), Electoral Commission of South Africa, http://www.elections.org.za/content/Elections/National-and-provincial-elections-results/.

2   Ibid.

3   Ibid.

4   IRR: *South Africa Survey 2012*, Johannesburg, 2012, p. 799.

5   Ibid.

6   Van Onselen, G: "The ANC: Fight Club", *Politicsweb,* 6 July 2012, http://www.politicsweb.co.za/politicsweb/view/politicsweb/ en page71619?oid=310629&sn=Detail&pid=71619.

7   Address by Zwelinzima Vavi on his appointment as chairperson of the National Anti-Corruption Forum, 10 December 2012, http://www.cosatu.org.za/show.php?ID=6779.

8   Sapa: "Political murders: It's about money", 29 July 2012, *IOL News,* http://www.iol.co.za/news/politics/political-murders-it-s-about-money-1.1351279.

9   Johnson, RW: *South Africa: The First Man, The Last Nation.* Johannesburg: Jonathan Ball, 2006, p. 221.

10   Constitution of the African National Congress, as amended and adopted at the 53rd National Conference at Mangaung, Mangaung, 2012, http://www.anc.org.za/show.php?id=10177.

11   Nzimande, B: "What is the National Democratic Revolution?", *Umsebenzi Online*, Vol. 5, No. 66, 18 October 2006, http://www.sacp.org.za/main.php?ID=1850.

12   The Path to Power: Programme of the South African Communist Party, as adopted at the Seventh Congress of the SACP, 1989, http://www.sacp.org.za/docs/history/power1989.html.

13   Discussion by RW Johnson, I Filatova, A Jeffery, P Hoffman, and D Steward during a conference entitled National Policy at the Crossroads, Johannesburg Country Club, 25 July 2012. Organised by the FW de Klerk Foundation.

14   "The second transition? Building a national democratic society and the balance of forces in 2012", ANC discussion document towards the National Policy Conference, version 7.0 as amended by the Special NEC 27 February 2012, p. 35, http://www.anc.org.za/docs/discus/2012/transition.pdf.

15   Ibid., p. 40.

16   The Path to Power. Programme of the South African Communist Party.

17   Our Future: Make It Work, National Development Plan.

18   IRR: *South Africa Survey 2012*, Johannesburg, 2012, pp. 132-133.

19   Sapa: "Gordhan urges South Africans to save", *South Africa Info,* 14 July 2011, http://www.southafrica.info/news/business/715419.htm#.UqlWkOJOons.

20   IRR: *South Africa Survey 2012*, Johannesburg, 2012, pp. 132-133.

21   *Global Investment Trends Monitor*, UNCTAD, no date, http://unctad.org/en/Pages/

DIAE/Research%20on%20FDI%20and%20TNCs/Global-Investment-Trends-Monitor.aspx.

22 IRR: *South Africa Survey 2012*, Johannesburg, 2012, p. 174.

23 IRR: *South Africa Survey 2013*, Johannesburg, 2013, p. 205, Economic and financial indicators, *The Economist*; 4 January 2014, http://www.economist.com/category/print-sections/economic-and-financial-indicators.

24 Ibid.

25 Martins, B: "Response by the Minister of Transport to Question 1563", *Hansard*, 10 June 2011.

26 King, D (ed.): *Seventh Annual State of Logistics Survey for South Africa 2010*. Pretoria: CSIR Built Environment, February 2011, http://www.csir.co.za/sol/docs/7th_SoL_2010_March.pdf.

27 IRR: *South Africa Survey 2012*, Johannesburg, 2012, p. 359.

28 Esterhuizen, I: "Xstrata-Merafe venture shuts furnaces to help Eskom", *Mining Weekly*, 17 February 2012, http://www.miningweekly.com/article/xstrata-merafe-venture-shuts-furnaces-to-help-eskom-2012-02-17.

29 IRR: *South Africa Survey 2010/2011*, Johannesburg, 2011, p. 400.

30 Ibid., p. 325.

31 IRR: *South Africa Survey 2013*, Johannesburg, 2013, p. 353.

32 Ibid., pp. 178-190.

33 Various indicators by StatsSA, http://beta2.statssa.gov.za/; IRR: *South Africa Survey 2010/2011*, Johannesburg, 2011, p. 222.

34 IRR: *South Africa Survey 2010/2011*, Johannesburg, 2011, p. 220.

35 TNS Research Surveys: "Expect more flashpoints – half of SA's metro residents are still not satisfied with service delivery a year later", *Bizcommunity*, 2011, http://www.bizcommunity.com/PressOffice/PressRelease.aspx?i=157495&ai=48185.

36 IRR: *South Africa Survey 2012*, Johannesburg, 2012, pp. 106, 258.

37 IRR: *South Africa Survey 2010/2011*, Johannesburg, 2011, pp. 110-111.

38 IRR: *South Africa Survey 2012*, Johannesburg, 2012, p. 137.

39 Borkum, H: "Let's talk about parastatals, not nationalisation", *Business Report*, 5 July 2011, http://www.iol.co.za/business/news/let-s-talk-about-parastatals-not-nationalisation-1.1093264#.UqlsleJOons.

40 Gedye, L: "More tough love for parastatals", *Mail & Guardian*, 24 February 2012, http://mg.co.za/article/2012-02-24-more-tough-love-for-parastatals.

41 Centre for Development and Entreprise: "Job destruction in the South African clothing industry", press release on 29 January 2013, http://www.cde.org.za/joomlaorg/press-releases/87-press-releases/.

42 Leon, T: *On the Contrary: Leading the Opposition in a Democratic South Africa*. Johannesburg: Jonathan Ball, 2008, p. 617.

43 Sapa: "South Africa at corruption tipping point: Madonsela", *TimesLive*, 3 April 2012, http://www.timeslive.co.za/politics/2012/04/03/south-africa-at-corruption-tipping-point-madonsela.

44 Corruption Watch: "Public concern about corruption at 18-year high", 22 May

2012, http://www.corruptionwatch.org.za/content/public-concern-about-corruption-18-year-high.

45 IRR: *South Africa Survey 2013,* Johannesburg, 2013, p. 515.

46 Ibid., p. 532.

47 Ibid., p. 470.

48 Ibid., p. 256.

49 Development Indicators 2009, The Presidency, 2009; IRR: *South Africa Survey 2012,* Johannesburg, 2012, p. 807.

50 IRR: *South Africa Survey 2012,* Johannesburg, 2012, p. 813.

51 Ibid., p. 883.

52 Ibid., p. 809.

53 TNS Research Surveys: "Expect more flashpoints"; IRR: *South Africa Survey 2012,* Johannesburg, 2012, pp. 809-812.

54 IRR: *South Africa Survey 2012,* Johannesburg, 2012, pp. 317-320. As the terminology suggests, LSMs measure living standards, with scores ranging between 1 and 10. People at the lower end of the spectrum have lower standards of living, based on the assets they own, such as a cell phone or a vacuum cleaner. Those at the higher end of the spectrum have higher standards of living. Think of people in category 1 as desperately poor, and those in category 10 as relatively prosperous members of the middle classes, or better.

55 Sapa: "Mines will be nationalised: Malema", *IOLNews,* 9 October 2009, http://www.iol.co.za/news/politics/mines-will-be-nationalised-malema-1.461020#. Uql4xeJOons; Sapa: "Malema: What, me racist?", *News24,* 20 April 2011, http://www.news24.com/SouthAfrica/Politics/Malema-What-me-racist-20110420.

56 Higgs, N: "Most young South Africans feel the ANC decision to suspend Julius Malema for 5 years is justified", *Politicsweb,* 13 November 2011, http://www.politicsweb.co.za/politicsweb/view/politicsweb/en/page71619?oid=266484&sn=Detail&pid=71619.

57 Higgs, N: "38% of metro back mine nationalisation – TNS", *Politicsweb,* 11 April 2011, http://www.politicsweb.co.za/politicsweb/view/politicsweb/en/page71619?oid=230615&sn=Detail&pid=71619.

58 Higgs, N: "74% of metro adults think 'Kill the Boer/kill the farmer' counts as hate speech – TNS", *Politicsweb,* 24 April 2011, http://www.politicsweb.co.za/politicsweb/view/politicsweb/en/page71619?oid=230673&sn=Detail&pid=71619.

59 Mtyala, Q: "Take politics out of courts", *TimesLive,* 23 November 2012, http://www.timeslive.co.za/thetimes/2012/11/23/take-politics-out-of-courts-1.

60 Author unknown: "Nzimande slams 'judicial dictatorship' ", *City Press,* 17 December 2011, http://www.citypress.co.za/news/nzimande-slams-judicial-dictatorship-20111217/.

61 Author unknown: "South Africa: Vote on Protection of Information Bill damaging", *Human Rights Watch,* 22 November 2011, http://www.hrw.org/news/2011/11/22/south-africa-vote-protection-information-bill-damaging.

62 Development Indicators 2009, The Presidency, 2009; IRR: *South Africa Survey 2013,* Johannesburg, 2013, p. 716.

63 IRR: *South Africa Survey 2013,* Johannesburg, 2013, p. 735.

64 IRR: *South Africa Survey 2012*, Johannesburg, 2012, p. 666.

65 Mobile cellular subscriptions (per 100 people), The World Bank, no date, http://data.worldbank.org/indicator/IT.CEL.SETS.P2.

66 IRR: *South Africa Survey 2012*, Johannesburg, 2012, p. 662.

67 South African Audience Research Foundation (SAARF): *All Media Products Survey 2010*, http://www.saarf.co.za; IRR: *South Africa Survey 2013*, Johannesburg, 2013, pp. 317-320.

68 IRR: *South Africa Survey 2013*, Johannesburg, 2013, pp. 11-17.

69 IRR: *South Africa Survey 2010/2011*, Johannesburg, 2011, p. 610; IRR: *South Africa Survey 2012*, Johannesburg, 2012, p. 5.

70 Human Development Report 2010, United Nations Development Program, 2010, http://hdr.undp.org/en/reports/global/hdr2010/; IRR: *South Africa Survey 2012*, Johannesburg, 2012, pp. 35-37.

71 IRR: *South Africa Survey 2013*, Johannesburg, 2013, p. 669.

72 Social Security and Health Care Financing, National Treasury, 2012; Development Indicators 2010, The Presidency, 2010; IRR: *South Africa Survey 2013*, Johannesburg, 2013, p. 645.

73 IRR: *South Africa Survey 2012*, Johannesburg, 2012, pp. 286-288.

74 Atud, V: "Nationalisation and black advancement", in J Evans (ed.), *Nationalisation*. Johannesburg: Free Market Foundation, 2011.

75 IRR: Fast Facts (forthcoming).

CHAPTER 7

1 Some readers may feel certain important factors have been omitted. For example, I have been criticised in the past for not introducing environmental issues. I omit them largely because I believe a ten-year period is too short for climate change to have a dramatic effect on the country. It does not really matter, though; as long as we introduce most of the factors and trends at work in South African society, no other trends would have the capacity to overwhelm their collective impact.

CHAPTER 8

1 I decided to use a road metaphor for the names of the scenarios in this book since it aligns with the highway, road sign, and road map terminology used to build the scenarios. In this, our best-case scenario, a wide open road of opportunities leads South Africans into a much better future.

CHAPTER 9

1 In this scenario, we are confronted with a narrow road as democratic freedoms are restricted even as South Africans become increasingly prosperous.

CHAPTER 10

1   This is the worst-case scenario where South Africans follow a bone-jarring route into poverty and desperation.

CHAPTER 11

1   The name for this scenario alludes to the controversial tolling of freeways around Johannesburg. In this future, ill-advised and counter-productive policy-making sees the ANC lose a future election.

INDEX